Keep It, Grow It,
Enjoy It, Bestow It

Keep It, Grow It, Enjoy It, Bestow It

◆

Wealth Secrets of the Truly Affluent

Mitchell S. Brill

iUniverse, Inc.

New York Bloomington Shanghai

Keep It, Grow It, Enjoy It, Bestow It
Wealth Secrets of the Truly Affluent

iUniverse books may be ordered through booksellers or by contacting:

iUniverse
1663 Liberty Drive
Bloomington, IN 47403
www.iuniverse.com
1-800-Authors (1-800-288-4677)

ISBN: 978-0-595-49492-7 (pbk)
ISBN: 978-0-595-61125-6 (ebk)

Printed in the United States of America

To my wonderful wife Robin—without whose help and companionship my life is not possible. And to my three children Morgan, Mia and Michael; I am grateful they are a part of my life.

Contents

Acknowledgements

Writing a book is not an individual event; it is a team sport! Although my name is on the cover of this book, many of the ideas I have expressed are not original; they are in the public domain. What is original is the way I explain them. I wish to thank the many people who have helped make this book a reality.

Thank you to my wife Robin, who was not only supportive in this endeavor, but was a great sounding board after reading many, many drafts of this book. To Michael Levin whose time, patience and hard work were greatly appreciated.

Thank you to the many people who read this book for content and style, offering both their time and expertise. I greatly appreciated the help of Risa Askenas, Jeffrey Benowitz, Vincent Blazewicz, Thomas Ciardella, Anthony DeStefano, Christopher Drake, Pamela Fedele, Joseph Guyton, Jennifer Lawlor, Robert Lax, Amy Marklin, Joan Martin, Michael Roma, Michael Savino, Leslee Schwartz, Jeffrey Slevin, Denise Weiss, Michael Weiss and Lori Wolf.

Introduction

Bill and Jim were college roommates and the best of friends. Since they had not seen each other for a number of years, they decided to take a fishing trip. It was a beautiful Sunday morning and the lake was gorgeous. Bill was using a fishing lure his father had taught him how to make. Jim was using a lure he bought in a store. Bill caught fish after fish using his magic lure. Each time Bill pulled up a fish, he measured it. If the fish was less than eight inches, Bill threw it back; if it was more than twelve inches, Bill threw it back.

This went on for several hours until finally Jim said to Bill, "You know, I don't get it. You've had tremendous success fishing with that lure, but every time you catch a big fish you throw it back. Why is that?" Bill replied that he had fished with his father many times. His father only kept the fish that were between eight and twelve inches long. He admitted that he was not really sure why his father threw back the rest of the fish.

The next weekend when Bill saw his dad, he said, "I went fishing with Jim last week and every time I caught a fish that was more than twelve inches long, I threw it back. When Jim asked why, I explained to him that that was exactly what you did when we went fishing when I was a kid. Why did you do that Dad?" Bill's father smiled and said, "You know son, that's interesting. I did it because our frying pan was twelve inches in diameter. Obviously, any bigger fish wouldn't fit. However, I am not so sure why *you* did it." Bill was dumb-founded.

I tell this story to demonstrate that there are things we do in our lives without understanding them or stopping to consider why we do them. Sometimes we do things simply because that is what other people do. The fact that other people do things a particular way does not make it right or wrong for us. It just means that we do things without thinking and sometimes without reason. The lure Bill's dad taught him to make was effective and successful. Clearly, the lure is something Bill should continue to use. However, throwing the fish back according to the size of his dad's frying pan obviously makes no sense. The same is true of our financial plans. Typically, people do things because that is what everyone else is doing or because it is the way they have been doing it for years. In and of itself, this is not sound financial reasoning. This story illustrates the reasons why I wrote this book.

This book is about money and how to maximize the life you live. It is about achieving financial balance through financial strategies and the reasons why you need an efficient plan and a great financial strategist. This book is also about financial freedom and why traditional "needs-based" planning cannot provide the freedom you deserve. This book reveals what makes a plan great and how to create a plan that is ideal for you.

By examining the reasoning behind some of the financial decisions you make, this book will help you decide whether or not—and if necessary, how—to reevaluate your decision-making process.

Part 1:
Why Plan?

The answer is simple. Plan so that you can live better and have less stress about money. Plan so that you can live the best life possible. A great plan will give you the financial freedom to do the things you want to do—whether it is to live a certain lifestyle, pay for your children's educations or create a legacy for your family. Who needs to plan? Everyone, from the low-income earner to the truly affluent—especially the truly affluent. If you think that you do not need to plan because you are affluent and earn a very nice living, think again. The affluent need to plan even more; even the richest need planning. Think of it this way—the rich have more to lose. For those in the affluent segment of society, simple mistakes can have a greater overall impact on their wealth and on the wealth of their heirs.

What The Affluent Fear The Most

F. Scott Fitzgerald wrote, "Let me tell you about the very rich. They are different from you and me." No matter how the rich came into their money, they nevertheless have a common fear: the fear of losing what they have.

The affluent come by their wealth in a variety of ways. Some are entrepreneurs and build highly successful businesses. Others make their money on Wall Street or in their professions. Still others rise to high levels in corporate America, and some inherit their wealth. No matter how they come by their money, well-to-do individuals share that one basic fear: *losing what they have.*

For those at the top of the economic ladder, life is indeed sweet. Those on the top rung are living the American dream of creating and enjoying great wealth. They live in the best neighborhoods and their children attend, or will attend, the best schools. They belong to the best clubs and when they travel, only the best hotels and spas will do.

Yet the common fear that their wealth will go away can turn the dream they live into something of a nightmare. The fear of losing their wealth can turn into daily stress. They do not want to be forced to downsize their lifestyles. They do not want to trade in their luxury car for an economy car or swap their beautiful home for an apartment. They do not want to give up their memberships to the country clubs because they can no longer afford them. In short, the fear of losing what has taken them so long to attain can impede the enjoyment of their day-to-day life.

The problem for most affluent individuals is that while they are world-class within the sphere in which they made their money, they suspect that they do not know the best ways to protect what they have and to make it grow. They turn to financial advisors, but they have the nagging—and all too often correct—sense that most financial planners are simply not able to serve the needs of the affluent individual. There are several reasons for this.

First, most financial planners work from a "needs-based" model that I will discuss in later chapters. That model may arguably be appropriate for an individual making $40,000 or $50,000 a year, but certainly has no bearing on the financial life of an individual making half a million dollars a year, one million dollars a year, or more. Second, the affluent recognize that financial planners are often tied to particular financial products and thus lack the ability to think creatively about strategies that do not involve those particular products. Finally, most financial planners, accountants and other advice-givers are fixated on the idea of reducing taxes in the short-term without giving proper thought to the eventual tax "bite" that will occur years or even decades later. Financial planning is an ongoing activity, not a "set-it and forget it" exercise.

The affluent individual or couple often feels that "advisors" are giving biased, self-serving or shortsighted advice without taking into account the true goals of the individual. I define those goals as follows:

• To protect an individual's net worth,

• To permit an individual to live on as much money as possible now and in the future, and

- To pass on the maximum amount of wealth possible to the next generation or generations.

The affluent sense, quite accurately, that *the world as we know it is created to separate them from their wealth*. Any affluent individual will tell you that it is harder and harder to find good investments. The stock market has treaded water for years, bonds offer a relatively low rate of return and real estate, a relatively illiquid investment in the best of times, may be overheated and headed for a correction.

At the same time, despite the protestations of Washington, taxes keep rising, especially for high-income individuals. The cost of living continues to gallop forward and we all experience "sticker shock" every time we go to the supermarket, let alone each time we shop for a new car. The cost of high-end consumer goods like luxury cars, clothing and home furnishings continues to rise at a pace that almost certainly outstrips what the government claims to be the inflation rate.

Today, people in many businesses and professions are finding it harder and harder to generate income. The existence of the Internet has exacerbated a trend toward commoditization. This means that the market is judging more and more products and services strictly on price instead of any other criteria. If somebody else can do it cheaper than you, the market does not care that you do a better job. Today, people care only about the bottom line.

It gets worse. The government makes the rules and then changes the rules to its benefit. These changes are numerous and certainly never to the benefit of the individual. Financial institutions play fast and loose with investors taking an attitude into the marketplace of "catch me if you can." The financial pages are filled with reports of brokerage houses and investment firms—even those with the finest reputations—entering into multi-million dollar settlements with regulators rather than pleading guilty to shady practices that take advantage of the very people whose money they have the responsibility to protect.

On top of that, the individual has a limited time frame—a matter of decades or sometimes even just years—until big bills come due: college education for children, retirement and the high cost of health care for oneself or for one's parents. As a country song once put it, "Every time I try to make ends meet, they up and move the ends."

The affluent recognize that no one is going to express great sadness for them. After all, they are the ones with the highest net worths, the highest incomes and the highest standards of living. Yet *the affluent are grossly underserved when it comes to financial planning.* Nevertheless, the affluent fear, and rightly so, that unless they get the right advice, they will lose their wealth. If they are unable to maximize their income and net worth, they will not be able to maintain the lifestyle that they have come to enjoy, and they will not be able to pass on to their children and grandchildren the level of wealth that they might have wished for them to inherit.

If this sounds at all familiar to you, this is where I come in. As a financial strategist serving the affluent, I have the privilege of helping wealthy individuals, couples and families achieve their true financial goals without fear. I teach them how to preserve their capital, invest it wisely and safely and live on the maximum amount of money they can today, while passing on as much money as possible at some point in the future—without that grievous "bite" from Uncle Sam.

My clients report that my work with them has enhanced their lifestyles, protected their families and helped them achieve their goals with simplicity, balance and focus. The purpose of this book is to share with you some of the strategies and ideas that I share with my highly affluent and successful clientele. When people ask what separates me from others who also seek to serve the highly affluent, I explain that I take a macroeconomic, or long-term, view of an individual's entire financial life. I do not limit my examination to one product or one part of their plan. I put my clients into products and services that are best for them irrespective of the commission payable.

The comments I get from traditional financial planners who try to liken the services they provide to the comprehensive economic planning that I do are always the same—"I ask a lot of questions too," they say. And I always respond, "But do you really take into account every aspect of a client's financial life when you create their plan?"

I have heard "planners" say, "What does car insurance or home insurance have to do with a client's financial picture?" The answer is simple: if someone has the wrong kind of car insurance and they accidentally kill someone with their car, the fact that they have the "perfect financial plan" may be for naught because their financial life could be ruined.

As you will learn in this book, seemingly inconsequential items like these can have an enormous impact on preserving and protecting your financial freedom. Therefore, I see myself—and more importantly, my clients see me—as the individual in this field who truly understands the special requirements of the highly affluent, not the "planner" trying to sell them products and services that they may not need or that may not fit into their financial world.

I hope you enjoy all of the short essays you read in this book. My essays cover a wide variety of issues together with strategies and tactics for preserving and enhancing your wealth, protecting your lifestyle, ensuring a very comfortable retirement and protecting your estate from the onslaught of taxes and other factors that, over time, will erode your wealth if you are not cognizant of them. Let's get started.

Part 2:
How Financial Decisions
Are Made Today

Money and discussions about money evoke very strong feelings. As a result, we often make decisions about our money based on emotion instead of logic or economic reality. When financial decisions are made emotionally (with fear and trepidation, greed, false information, false memories and based on past performance), we often pay a huge financial price. Let's look at some of these decision-making forces and try to escape their hold and burst their mythical powers.

If I Feel Like A Million, How Come I'm Broke?

In a 1994 study Morningstar, a company that tracks and rates mutual funds, reported that they tracked 199 mutual funds from 1988 to 1994, a time that was very good for market returns. Morningstar reported that the mutual funds they tracked gained an average of approximately twelve percent per year, while the average investor during that same period averaged approximately a two percent per year gain.

How is it possible that the funds performed so much better than the average investor?

The simple answer is that people, reacting to financial news, did the exact opposite of the famous Charles Dow maxim "buy low, sell high." Instead, they bought at whatever the market price was, and then they sold low. In fact, they sold so low that they missed out on most of the gains—precisely eighty percent of the gains—that the mutual funds enjoyed.

The easiest way to understand this point is to think back to the stock market crash of 1987. On Monday, October 19, 1987, the Dow Jones Industrial Average fell 508.32 points, erasing twenty-two percent of the value of the Dow. Many people, fearing the worst (and engaging in an emotional, knee-jerk reaction), pulled their money out of stocks and mutual funds in the days and weeks following the crash. Nevertheless, the market returned to pre-crash levels within just two years of the crash. Plenty of people who invested after the crash, sensing accurately that a fire sale was going on, made out like bandits.

Acting emotionally is understandable. Again, the biggest fear of many successful individuals is that they might lose their lifestyle—the socioeconomic level of material goods and the social status that they enjoy. When the stock market is crashing and a large portion of wealth seemingly vanishes in the course of one bleak business day, it is understandable that emotions take over. Yet those who take a more rational approach and hold or even buy in the aftermath of a crash, make money. Those who react based on emotion lose out big time.

The lesson to be learned from the history of the stock market is that investing in the market is a long-term proposition. People lose money when they pull it out of the market for emotional reasons which are not based on a predetermined or scientific plan. Thus, when you begin to invest, you should understand what you are looking for as far as your return and you should stick to the plan you made to get there. You cannot panic at the bumps in the road along the way. Bumps should be anticipated and planned for.

My Memories Of The Depression (Even Though I Wasn't There)

Consider this: the Great Depression of the 1930s has a more powerful effect on the children and grandchildren of those who lived through the Depression than it did on those individuals who were adults living through it. The "Depression mentality," also known as "scarcity thinking," is an extremely powerful factor in the financial lives of the generations that followed the Depression generation. Those of us who grew up with parents or grandparents who lived through the 1930s learned about the Depression not by experiencing it as adults but instead *by hearing about it as children.* Therefore, we did not have an adult mind to filter the facts from the fantasy.

Let me offer my own personal family history as an example. When I was growing up, we frequently traveled to Florida to visit my grandparents who were married during the Depression. Each time we went, my grandfather took me aside and showed me the money that he had tucked away in the family Bible. He would tell me that the money in the Bible, and the house in which he and my grandmother lived, would all belong to my siblings and me someday. He also wanted to make sure that I was mindful of the possibility that a worldwide crash could come again at any time.

When you are a child and your grandparent tells you that the sky may fall, you believe it. I do not think my experience is unique among people my age. We learned about the Depression not by our own experience, but by hearing about it in ways that made us conjure up this terrifying boogeyman when we were too small to make sense of it and too scared to think rationally about it. Alternatively, when you are an adult and someone tells you that the sky is falling, you can assess the situation yourself.

Could there be another worldwide depression? Anything is possible, especially given the instabilities that exist in this "Age of Terror." Is it likely that the world banking system and the world economy will falter to that extent? No. Today there are many more safeguards to prevent such a downturn. Yet the childhood experience of the story of the Depression dictates, to a much greater degree than many of us realize, the way we feel about money and the way we act with regard to investing. I am not minimizing the painful experiences of those who actually lived through the Depression. I am merely suggesting that the adults who survived the Depression may have a more balanced view about the future of the world's economic system than their children and grandchildren.

Fear Leads To Inefficiency

The number one fear people have is that they will run out of money. This is especially true for those entering their retirement years.

"Running out of money," means different things to different people. For the most part, we are not talking about having zero dollars in the bank. Instead, for the affluent, "running out of money" means being unable to live in the style to which they have become accustomed. It means that they will not have enough money to sustain their membership at the club or to repair or replace their Mercedes. They imagine themselves trying to explain to their friends why they left the country club or why they turned in the Jaguar and bought a fuel-efficient, cost-cutting Hyundai.

The problem is that the fear of losing everything often causes people to do nothing. I frequently encounter affluent individuals who are so afraid of making a mistake with their money that they become paralyzed and do nothing at all. Doing nothing with money often means leaving it in a savings account where it earns about four percent interest per year. In a time when inflation is running at three percent, if you are getting just four percent interest on your money in a savings account and that four percent is really reduced to two percent after taxes, you are actually moving backwards at a rate of one percent per year. It is not uncommon for me to meet individuals who have hundreds of thousands to several million dollars sitting in savings accounts, losing one percent per year to inflation, simply because they are afraid to do something with that money for fear of making a mistake.

There is no doubt that fear leads to inefficiency. The other side of the fear coin is greed. Fear causes people to fail to allocate any of their money at all to the proper investments because they are afraid of losing it. Greed causes people to contribute to the wrong investments or to stay too long in what were once the right investments, because they are always looking for a bigger return. For me, efficiency means finding an appropriate mix of investments that not only meet an individual's level of risk tolerance, but that also beat inflation after taxes.

Doing nothing is not an option. Mark Twain once said, "A cat that sits on a hot stove will never sit on another stove again, hot or cold." You might have gotten singed or even burned with previous investments, quite possibly in the market's "dot-com" crash. This does not mean, however, that it is okay to stick your assets in a savings account and allow inflation to eat away at them. There are no guarantees in life. However, if you are willing to heed good advice, your likelihood of driving that Hyundai past the country club where you used to belong … is very slim.

Chicken Little Is Alive And Well

Chicken Little was wrong—the sky is not falling and it is not going to fall. But that does not mean that he still does not have tens of millions of devoted followers.

In an era of uncertainty like ours, it is dangerous not to consider the fact that bad things can happen in the world. The problem is that too many people allow their thinking to be dominated by negativity and fear. This kind of thinking is called scarcity thinking. The problem with scarcity thinking is that if you are looking for scarcity, you are going to find it.

Simply put, what you focus on expands. If you focus on scarcity and negativity, chances are that you will achieve just that. Conversely, if you seek abundance and have a positive outlook you are more likely to find abundance.

How does this really play out? When people have the attitude that the sky could fall at any time, they become too cautious. They actually increase their risk while trying to avoid risk by failing to act or by placing all of their investment eggs in one basket. It is true that a generation ago, individuals did well by buying and holding shares in large, traditional companies like IBM or the telephone company. Today, keeping all of your assets in one stock is a recipe for disaster. Bad things can, and often do, happen to companies. We cannot predict the future in any field. For instance, we do not know how competition (domestic or international), weather, economy, technology, energy or politics will affect any one company. To place all of your money into a single investment, in an effort to avoid risk, actually increases risk.

An investment philosophy based on a mentality of scarcity is not likely to produce money. Instead, it is likely to produce more scarcity.

It Is Tough To Repeat

In professional sports, it is very difficult for a team to win a championship, come back the next year, and win another one. It happens so infrequently that when a team actually wins two championships in a row, everyone starts wondering if we are looking at a "dynasty." It is no different in the investment world. It is very hard for a champion to repeat. Yet when a particular mutual fund, investment manager or stock has a very good year, that is where everybody seems to place his or her money the next year. It is virtually impossible to be the best year after year after year. So when we place a bet on last year's winner, we are almost inevitably looking at a team that will not win, place or even show this year.

For example, a 2006 Fidelity study of nine key market indices examined a twenty year period and suggested that if you had invested in the index that represented last year's winner, you would have made far less money than you would have had you spread your investment evenly throughout the nine indices. Ironically, betting on last years' winner is almost a surefire way to lose.

Is There A Place For Greed In Your Portfolio?

The Internet bubble wiped out trillions of dollars of wealth from otherwise intelligent, rational investors because they followed the herd. They stopped following the path of sound financial investing and looked to the short cut that greed offered.

There may be, however, a place for greed in the average investor's portfolio. It is possible that some of your total portfolio ought to be in highly speculative, highly risky investments that have the possibility of providing spectacular returns. A small portion, however, should be the limit—less for some people, slightly more for others. The problem with the Internet frenzy is that people were devoting forty percent, sixty percent, or even their entire portfolio to greed-based investing with predictably disastrous consequences.

Here is a true tale of woe from the Internet bubble era: a client of mine received shares of tech stock from her father in trust for her son's college education. This particular company had a spectacular rise during the tech boom of the 1990's. My client rode that stock up from a value of a few thousand dollars in early 1995 to over $200,000 in less than five years. In a meeting I told her, "It's the bottom of the ninth, two outs … the Yankees are up by four … and Mariano Rivera, at the time, the best closer in baseball, is coming in. You've got your child's college education paid for if you don't screw it up. Get out! Take your winnings off the table!"

I met with that same client in 2002. "How did you do with that stock?" I asked her. "It's your fault!" the client snarled at me. "You should have told me to get out! The stock tanked. I gave back all the gains," she reported. "I did tell you to get out!" I replied. "Don't you remember? Bottom of the ninth! Up by four! Rivera coming in from the bullpen!" The look on her face told me that she did in fact remember our conversation. Suddenly she remembered my warning all too well. Not that she heeded it.

I had to ask. "Why didn't you sell the stock?" I needed this insight into her psyche if I was going to serve her better. She shrugged. "I didn't want to pay the tax on the gains," she admitted, ruefully. "And now the thing is worth less than when I got it."

Traditional thinking dictates that the more risk you take, the better your return will be. This simply is not true. A superior and efficient strategy is one that gets you a high return. Risk has a nasty downside—you might lose some or all of your money! That is why they call it *risk!* There is a place for greed in your portfolio. But it cannot drive all of your thinking.

To illustrate this point, consider the following scenario:

Sally earns $500,000 per year for thirty years. Over that period of time she spends thirty percent of her income on taxes ($150,000), twenty percent of her income on debt

($100,000), and forty percent of her income is consumed by her lifestyle ($200,000). This leaves ten percent of her income ($50,000) to save in an investment vehicle at six percent after taxes. At the end of thirty years Sally will have an account containing $4,190,083 (see Figure 2.1).

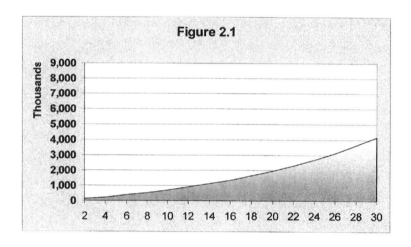

Now, lets say that Sally takes on more risk and is successful. Remember, Sally *could* lose. Nevertheless, as a result of the gamble, Sally manages to increase her rate of return to eight percent after taxes from six percent in the previous example. At the end of the same thirty-year period, Sally will have an account containing $6,117,293. That figure represents $1,927,210 more than she had at six percent (see figure 2.2).

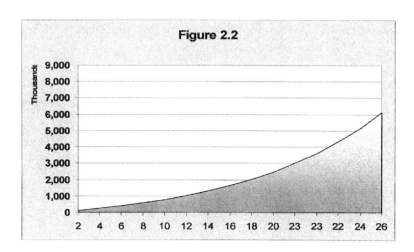

Finally, let's assume Sally achieves the same six percent after-tax rate of return that she achieved in the first example, and instead of taking on more risk, she uses a superior strategy which allows her to lower her taxes and her debt by a combined ten percent of her salary. In this scenario, at the end of the thirty-year period, Sally will have $8,380,167 in the same account. Sally would have two times as much money as she had in the first low-risk example and $2,262,874 more than she had in the second example where her risk was greater (see figure 2.3).

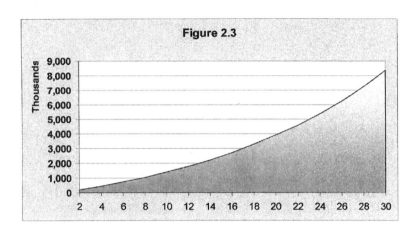

The moral to Sally's story is that superior and efficient strategies have a better overall rate of return than strategies that focus on simply getting a slightly higher return on your money. If you can get better results without taking on more risk, why wouldn't you do it?

Everybody Lies About Money

Everybody lies, especially when it comes to his or her investments.

How do I know this is true? Ask yourself this simple question: Have you ever heard anyone at your club, at a social organization or at a cocktail party say, "Boy, I got killed in the market!"

The simple fact is that people usually talk about their winning investments, not about their losing investments. It is one thing if you are sitting down with your best friend and talking candidly about your experiences in the market. But when people are in social settings, the pressure is so intense to look like a winner, talk like a winner and sometimes unfortunately, brag like a winner.

Think about people you know who go to Las Vegas or Atlantic City on a regular basis. You always seem to hear about the time they won a lot of money. Chances are, however, that they will never tell you about the ten or twelve other trips when they came away with their tails between their legs.

The net effect of all these lies is that the people hearing these stories think, "I am a loser! Everybody else is making a lot of money, and I am getting left behind!" In an effort to become more successful they end up taking more chances than they would have otherwise taken or should have taken under normal circumstances, all in an effort to keep up with the impression the Joneses are making. The Joneses may not be any better off than you are, but they sure talk a good game.

Buying into the lies that people tell about their investment success leads to uninformed decisions and, consequently, the loss of money. There is no universal discount rate to apply to the stories you hear. Ask yourself this question the next time someone is bragging about one of their investment successes: When was the last time you ever heard them talk about losing money? Is it possible that they are right one hundred percent of the time?

Everybody lies! Do not let other people's lies convince you to make inappropriate financial decisions.

Why The Rich Get Richer

For the wealthy, money is no object. For the middle class, money is no subject.

The simple fact is that wealthy people talk about money far more often than people in the middle-class. If you grew up in a wealthy home chances are you heard your parents talking about investments and they quite likely shared financial information with you. They might have had you pick out a stock to buy when you were still a child. The wealthy also have more opportunities to talk about investments. From a cultural point of view, if you are a member of the highly affluent class in American society, it is perfectly acceptable for you to be out on the golf course at the club with a friend or business associate talking about investments. This is one way the rich get richer—because they talk about money with each other, with their friends and with their children.

It really does take money to make money. When you are affluent and surrounded by other affluent people, you have access to better investment options. You can get into deals that the rest of the world will never even hear about. It is considerably easier to take twenty million dollars and turn it into forty million than it is to take five hundred thousand dollars and turn it into one million dollars.

By contrast, in middle-class homes money is often a taboo subject. Discussion of money matters does not occur at the family dinner table. Fears, concerns and ambiguous attitudes about money are often transferred from parents to children, instead of real information about how money works or how to attain it. This is one of the greatest advantages that wealthy families have over middle-class families—their willingness to talk about money.

My advice to my clients is always to involve their children in the world of investment and finance. Explain to your children how the stock market works or how a particular investment or financial product should be used. Your children do not have to know your net worth or your specific investments; however, it does make sense to allow money to be a subject for healthy discussions at the dinner table.

My Junk Drawer

My sock drawer is meticulously organized. There are no stray socks, no socks with holes and no balls of socks that do not match. I can reach into my sock drawer every business morning and pull out a pair of perfectly clean, perfectly respectable, perfectly matched socks.

Now, if we go downstairs and visit the junk drawer in the kitchen, it would be a different story. My junk drawer is a huge mess. In my junk drawer you will find (unless you need it at that very moment) a hammer, a pair of scissors, some spark plugs, washers, a mismatched set of wrenches, and two-thirds of the implements you need to hang a picture on a wall. In short, my junk drawer is full of junk. Nothing matches, nothing works together and the presence of any given item in the drawer is purely random.

You might ask why I am talking about a sock drawer and a junk drawer in a book about financial strategies. For most people, their financial planning has a lot more in common with my junk drawer than it does with my sock drawer. People buy various financial products—a mortgage, insurance, mutual funds, retirement plans—and stuff them all in the equivalent of a financial junk drawer, not asking themselves if the purchases make sense, if they work well together or if they are even necessary in the first place. This kind of uncoordinated financial planning barely deserves the title "planning." Buying financial products, even good ones, in a helter-skelter manner leads to inefficiency and does not get us any closer to reaching our goals. Why do we do this? Why do so many of us have an investment and financial portfolio that looks more like a junk drawer than a well-organized sock drawer?

There are many reasons. Often we buy a particular financial product because "everyone else is doing it." We hear at the club, the gym or the barbershop, that a lot of people are "getting into" a particular stock, form of insurance or type of mortgage. But it really comes back to the question that your mother used to ask you: "If Johnny jumped off a bridge, would you?" "But Johnny did it" did not work as a justification for random behavior then, and it certainly does not work as a justification for random financial decisions now.

Peer pressure is not the only reason why so many of us end up with financial junk drawers. Ask yourself this: when a financial institution is offering you an investment, who bears the risk—you or the financial institution? Your objectives and those of the financial institutions are diametrically opposed. The financial institutions want you to give them your money on a regular basis. They would like to hold onto your money for as long as possible so that they can make as much money, using your money, as they can. In return, they would like to give you back as little money as possible.

Basically, if a financial institution is offering you an investment, chances are that you, and not the financial institution, bear most, if not all, of the risk. The conventional wisdom about risk is that the more risk you take, the more money you will make—nothing ventured, nothing gained. Yet success actually consists of managing your risk strategically. Often, less money invested in the right places at lower risk allows you to live on more money and pass on more to your heirs. Does your financial future look more like a sock drawer or a junk drawer? Only you can answer that question.

Stop Getting Advice From Magazines Driven By Advertising

If you read popular financial magazines on a regular basis, you will see that they regularly run articles proclaiming the ten best mutual funds to own. The problem is that the list keeps changing. If these funds are really so great, why would they ever slip off of the "ten best" list? Does the constant change in the "ten best" list mean that you should continually revise your holdings so that it mirrors the new list?

The reason why these magazines keep changing the "ten best" list is purely economic. The magazines want to sell more copies; a new list presents new reasons to buy subsequent issues of a magazine. Therefore, the advice given in these financial magazines is not completely reliant on the condition of the market.

These magazines' style of advising brings to mind Woody Allen's joke about stockbrokers: "They invest your money ... until there's nothing left."

Additionally, these magazines consistently publish articles about the difference between term insurance and whole life insurance and consistently recommend term insurance. They advise their readers to buy term insurance instead of whole life insurance and invest the difference. Again, the simple answer is that the advertisers in these magazines are mutual funds. If the typical financial magazine is telling you to buy term and invest the difference, where are you most likely to invest the difference? That's right—in mutual funds. These magazines are simply not going to make a recommendation that would violate the best interests of their most important advertisers.

Furthermore, you see the cover story on these magazines every so often: "Where is the best place to put ten thousand dollars now?" If you open up the magazine, you will see the latest and greatest investment ideas from the editors. The problem is that the editors are suggesting that you take that entire ten thousand dollars and put it in one place. When you do that, you have an unbalanced portfolio—and an unbalanced portfolio means too much risk.

Where is the best place to put $10,000 anytime? Diversify the money among a group of different assets. Put some in your qualified plan—your IRA or your 401(k) plan. Put some in stocks and bonds and put some in separately managed accounts. You cannot have a successful basketball team without diversity—nobody is going to win with five point guards. The same thing is true with investing.

Financial magazines, like any other magazines, are beholden to their advertisers. That explains why their advice rarely strays from suggesting that you put money into vehicles created by their advertisers, regardless of how much risk you bear by keeping all of your eggs in one basket.

Just Because The Newspaper Said So …

Not long ago, a newspaper I read ran an article on an investment vehicle called the variable annuity, condemning it as a complete rip-off. The newspaper discovered some variable annuities with high management fees and high surrender charges and came to the conclusion that all variable annuities must be bad and that none of its readers should ever go near them.

Let's take a look at what a variable annuity is and see if what the newspaper determined has any basis in reality. A variable annuity is an investment offered by insurance companies that grows tax-deferred. It is a collection of mutual funds in which an insurance company can invest on your behalf. When you purchase a variable annuity, you are simply buying mutual funds—but you are buying them with the enormous buying power of a huge, successful insurance company, and you are buying them with the substantial wisdom of the investment team working at that insurance company. I talk numerous times in this book about how individual investors make decisions based on their emotions and not upon facts. Investment experts at the insurance companies are anything but emotional when it comes to making decisions. Not only do they have access to information that the rest of us do not have, they simply do a better job of making investment decisions than the average investor. So when you buy a variable annuity, in essence, you are buying mutual funds in a way that can increase your tax advantage and minimize your risk.

You can buy a variable annuity with before-tax or after-tax dollars. This means that you can buy a variable annuity by writing a check or by using money in a qualified plan like a 401(k) plan or an IRA. In either case, you only pay taxes when you start withdrawing money from the annuity. Accordingly, the annuity is a tax-deferred investment.

There are a number of ways to get your money out of a variable annuity. For example, starting at age fifty-nine and one-half, you can "surrender" the variable annuity; that is, you can return it to the insurance company and receive all of the money that it has accumulated for you. Or you can "annuitize the annuity." This is a fancy way of saying that you can turn your variable annuity into an income stream for a period of time that you choose. For example, you can tell the insurance company, "pay me an income stream for the rest of my life." Or you can say, "pay us an income stream for the length of my life plus my spouse's life." Annuitization is a pretty powerful tool. You can use it to guarantee an income stream which will prevent you from running out of money during your lifetime.

The downside to variable annuities is that you tie up your money. That is why I tell my clients that a variable annuity is a long-term investment. Thus, money that is already socked away in a 401(k) plan, IRA, Keogh or other qualified plan is perfect for a variable annuity. The money is tied up anyway, so what's the difference? As long as you do not have access to it, let it really maximize its growth.

Many variable annuities provide other benefits in addition to lifetime income. For instance, they can allow the investor to diversify among many asset classes and rebalance their portfolio free of charge on a regular basis without having to baby-sit the investments. In many variable annuities the principal is guaranteed. Some variable annuities even have a minimum guaranteed rate of return allowing people to invest in the market thus participating in the market's upside while eliminating, or at least limiting, the market's downside. The investor gets a guaranteed return with no risk.

Although variable annuities are typically purchased by older investors, they may also be appropriate for many younger people who have begun to accumulate large amounts of money. Is it fair then for a newspaper to have said that variable annuities are appropriate for no one, simply because some, but certainly not all, variable annuities have high management fees and high surrender charges?

Interestingly enough, in the case of this particular newspaper article, a friend of mine asked the reporter who wrote the piece condemning variable annuities why she wrote the article. The reporter's answer was shocking. "They told me," she said, "to write a piece smearing variable annuities." I found this truly appalling. I understand the motivation of the newspaper. If they can find something negative to write, they have created some news. On the other hand, if they had written, "Variable annuities are a great thing!"—would a story like that sell papers? Negative press sells far more papers than positive press.

The correct headline should have been "Variable annuities may be appropriate for you." But that is boring. The newspaper I read was utterly irresponsible in its reporting on this investment vehicle. If variable annuities are so bad, and so bad for everyone, why do insurance commissioners in all fifty states approve them? Why do all of the most legitimate, respected, oldest and successful insurance companies in the United States offer them? If variable annuities are as horrendous as this article portrayed them to be, the article could have been titled, "Variable Annuities—a Scam Perpetrated by Insurance Companies and Supported by Insurance Commissioners." The truth is there is no scam and such an article would have been libelous.

What does this mean to you? It means that you simply cannot always trust what you read even in the most prestigious and reliable journalistic institutions. Newspapers are just that: journalistic. They are not financial institutions. You have got to do your own homework. You cannot buy into the mass consciousness about investing. Everybody is trying to sell you something. It makes a lot of sense to keep one hand on your wallet or purse while you use the other hand to make a phone call and check out something that you have read. Variable annuities are outstanding investments for a lot of people. Media coverage, which is sometimes based more on hype and spin than a desire for accuracy, is not doing you a favor.

Be aware of generalizations and sensational news stories; they may not apply to you. Just because many people in society believe something to be true does not make it so. Remember, at some point in the world's history it was widely accepted that the world was flat. We now know that is not the case. There is a difference between opinion and fact. Financial strategies should be proven to you with respect to your set of facts and circumstances before you accept them as true.

Call-In Shows In General

Not long ago, one of my clients called me very excited because he was watching Suze Ormon on TV and he thought she had given him a great investing idea. Without getting into the specifics of the particular investment idea, I can tell you that it was dead wrong for my client and other individuals like my client, who have high incomes and high net worths.

"Who calls in to Suze Ormon's show?" I asked.

"The average American" my client told me.

"And, who do you suppose that is?" I asked.

"People with around $40,000 a year in income," my client told me. "People with big debt, people paying off high student loans and credit card bills."

"Is that you?" I asked.

"Of course not," my client said.

"Then why are you looking to her for financial advice?"

The simple fact is that if you are making more than $500,000 a year, you are in the top one percent of earners in the United States.[1] TV financial entertainment shows like Suze Ormon's are simply not aimed at the top one or two percent. There are not enough viewers in that category to support a television show. In 2006, according to the United States Census Bureau, the median household income in the United States was $48,201.[2] Suze Ormon's show and shows with financial entertainers like her are aimed at the broad swath of the middle class, which may include people who have an income of $48,000 a year, heavy credit card debt and student loans to repay. If a person's financial position is so radically different from yours, why would you take advice from someone whose advice is geared specifically to people who earn one-tenth as much as you do?

I do not mean any disrespect towards Suze Ormon. I am sure she provides a valuable service to her target audience. But if you are a high income, high net worth individual, you might as well grab the remote and see what else is on. One Suze does not fit all.

Next Exit—100 Miles

When most people make investments they have entrance strategies, but seldom do they have exit strategies. They buy houses, stocks, bonds and collectibles or they put money into retirement plans. Rarely, however, have they thought through how and when they will exit those investments.

1.   U.S. Census Bureau News Release In Regards to Median Income, August 28, 2007.
2.   U.S. Census Bureau News Release In Regards to Median Income, August 28, 2007.

The key "exit strategy" question is this: How do I get my money out of a given investment or how can I pass it on to my heirs in the most tax-advantaged way?

It is a little like getting on a highway with no directions to your destination. You knew where the entrance ramp was. But do you know when to get off? The problem in the investment world is that often, if we miss an exit, we do not have the opportunity of backtracking in the other direction in order to get to the right exit. When we pass up an exit opportunity in the investment world, it may be gone forever.

You would never get on a highway knowing that there were no exits for the next hundred miles unless you knew for an absolute certainty that this was the right direction for you and that you would not need an earlier exit under any circumstance. It is great to know how to get into a given investment. But it is equally or perhaps even more important to know how and when to get out. You must have an exit strategy so that you are making decisions about your investments, instead of having decisions forced upon you.

The Sandwich Generation

The Baby Boom generation has a new name today—the Sandwich Generation, as they are facing two substantial financial responsibilities at the same time. Today, people in their forties and fifties often must pay for their children's college educations and their parents' health care ... at the same time. This double whammy makes it even more important for people in this position to have a plan.

You ... Who Are On The Road ... Must Have A Code ...

Remember Crosby, Stills, Nash and Young? What they sang in the 70s is just as true today. You have to have a code to live by and your money needs direction too! Planning is essential for anyone who wishes to create financial independence.

A financial plan is a roadmap to freedom. When you know your ultimate destination, your financial plan gives you a set of guidelines for decision-making along the way. Any new step in your financial plan should either help you reach your goal or it should not be taken.

Another vital benefit of a personal financial plan is coordination. When everything you do is coordinated, you, your plan and your investments will be more efficient. If your plan is efficient, you will have more money to spend and pass on to those you love.

What bears repeating is the goal I suggest to my clients: create more wealth so that you can spend more money in your lifetime and one day pass on more to your survivors. As financial products become more and more complex, the importance of a simple, clear, easy-to-understand plan becomes increasingly critical.

Part 3:
Why Today's "School" of Planning Does Not Work

Traditional financial planning is "needs-based." You sit down with a planner who asks you how much money you will need when you retire. The two of you then adjust that number according to an inflation rate—which is only a guess at what inflation will be over your lifetime. Given that number and the number of years until your retirement, your planner figures out how much money you will need to put away weekly, monthly, quarterly or yearly, with an average rate of return (which is also a guess) to get to your goal number.

Who Needs "Needs-Based" Planning? Nobody.

There are a myriad of problems inherent with the "needs-based" planning approach. First and foremost is that the formula is based entirely on unknown variables. Each variable in the equation is a guess. It may be based on past performance of the products considered; however, common knowledge dictates that "past performance is no guarantee of future results." It is impossible to expect that the formula will work out the same way twice, much less over a long period of time with all of the unknown variables. Who knows what inflation or the rate of return will be like in the future?

Moreover, even if the guesses at the average rate of return are correct, the formula will still fail because neither the inflation rate nor the rate of return will be constant. Thus, the order in which the rates occur will affect the outcome. For instance, lets examine a fifteen-year time horizon for two investment accounts. Both accounts start with $1,000,000 and achieve an average after tax rate of return of ten percent (see figures 3.1 and 3.2). Notice that the accounts yield far different results. Portfolio A yields $4,142,271 at the end of the fifteen years. Portfolio B yields $3,579,289—a difference of $562,982.

Figure 3.1

Year	Rate of Return Portfolio A	Account Value Portfolio A	Rate of Return Portfolio B	Account Value Portfolio B
1	15.00%	1,150,000	8.00%	1,080,000
2	10.00%	1,265,000	17.00%	1,263,600
3	4.00%	1,315,600	-15.00%	1,074,060
4	7.00%	1,407,692	20.00%	1,288,872
5	12.00%	1,576,615	2.00%	1,314,649
6	3.00%	1,623,913	5.00%	1,380,382
7	7.00%	1,737,587	25.00%	1,725,477
8	15.00%	1,998,226	-20.00%	1,380,382
9	9.00%	2,178,066	30.00%	1,794,496
10	8.00%	2,352,311	30.00%	2,332,845
11	11.00%	2,611,065	5.00%	2,449,488
12	15.00%	3,002,725	10.00%	2,694,436
13	13.00%	3,393,079	-10.00%	2,424,993
14	12.00%	3,800,249	20.00%	2,909,991
15	9.00%	4,142,271	23.00%	3,579,289
Average Annual Return		**10%**		**10%**
Ending Value		**4,142,271**		**3,579,289**

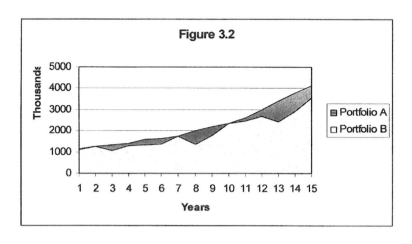

Figure 3.2

Additionally, things constantly change. Your needs change. Your health is never guaranteed. Your life expectancy changes according to how you live and how life treats you. Do you know how you want to live at age eighty? How will your personal values change over the next thirty, forty or fifty years? In fact, if you look back only twenty years ago, did you envision that you would be where you are now? Where will you be forty years from today? There is no way to answer these questions with any kind of certainty. Therefore, planning that is based on extrapolation from where you are today to where you think you will be in the future—based on unknown variables—cannot possibly be reliable.

What we think will happen in the future has little if any bearing on what actually happens. If we could see into the future, we could plan our lives to the dollar. We would have invested in Microsoft at the beginning. We cannot know for sure what taxes, inflation, life expectancy and health care will look like in the future. There are too many variables! Additionally, things can and do break, markets go up and down, taxes go up and inflation increases. You might get sued, the government can and will change the rules on retirement accounts and your portfolio might not perform as expected. Haven't there been enough unforeseen economic, natural and financial disasters in the last several years to teach us that we cannot plan only for the best scenarios? You must consider what would happen if things do not go the way that you had hoped or planned. Even if you could plan for an illness, could you possibly know the cost of the treatment ten or twenty years from now? On the flip side, with all of the technological advances in the last twenty years, how could you know what new things you will want and "cannot live without?" For instance, I used to own a record player, then I had an eight-track tape player and then I had a cassette player. There were no cell phones, DVD Players or iPods when I was a kid, and I could not have conjured them up in my wildest imagination.

The truth is that we do not live according to our needs anyway! Our wants play a huge part in our day-to-day lives. If we truly lived according to our needs, we would all lead a very minimalist life. We would all eat tuna fish or pasta three times a day and wear nothing but blue jeans (and not the expensive premium denim kind). You want to live nicely. You want to live according to your wants and desires. The best form of planning is creating a life plan that helps you reach an optimal level of spending and saving during your life, so that you can live life to the fullest the entire time you are actually alive.

The Best Things In Life Used To Be Free

You must have noticed that a lot of the things you never had to pay for in the past require money out of your pocket in today's world. Chances are when you were growing up, TV was free. Today we pay money for cable or direct TV. Granted, the selection of programming is more varied and arguably better, but you are still writing a check every month for a service you never paid for in the past. When you were growing up, did you ever imagine that you would be buying bottles of water in the supermarket because you did not trust, or simply disliked, the water coming out of your tap? It used to be free to call Directory Assistance—411—to get a phone number. Not anymore.

This reminds me of one of my favorite Seinfeld bits. Seinfeld is talking about how the older generation loves to discuss how cheap things were when they were growing up. Seinfeld quips, "Back then, a car costs a dime. A house, a quarter." Seinfeld then goes on to ask, "What are we going to tell our grandchildren? When we were young, dogs couldn't vote! They had no say at all! We kept them on leashes!" I doubt that dogs will ever get the right to vote. But, things do not only change in the Seinfeld world, they change in real life.

We have absolutely no way of predicting what things are going to cost as we age. It may be that some of the things that we take for granted as free today may have a very steep price tag in the future. The cost of items we never paid for before may increase so radically that we will be stunned by the amount of money we are paying for those previously free items. Certainly the cost of a college education gallops ahead of the inflation rate, as does the cost of health care. It is absolutely impossible to predict how expensive things are going to be by the time a need arises for you or a loved one.

Traditional "needs-based" financial planning rests on the assumption that whatever things cost today, they will cost essentially the same amount in the future, with some adjustment for a guessed rate of inflation. We know that this is not true. We also know that the inflation rate is different for everyone. The rising cost of the things that we actually use is different for each person. Take for instance—gasoline. Gas is a commodity. If I have an SUV and you have a hybrid, the rise and fall of the gas price will affect each of us very differently. So the real question is: why do so many of us put so much faith in traditional financial planning? I do not make those assumptions about my future and neither should you.

What If?

After "I'm broke," the words "what if" are the two words that the traditional financial planner dreads the most. This is because traditional financial planning is based on the idea that the world is going to stay pretty much the way it is forever. All of the basic assumptions the traditional planner makes about your life, the economy, the stock market and interest rates are assumed to hold true from the moment you make your financial plan until the day you write your last check.

Of course the only true constant in life is change. As the former Chairman of GE Jack Welch liked to say, we have to "eat change for breakfast." One of the many troubles with traditional financial planning is that it relies on a static economic model. If things change too much, your plan will not work. And as we all know, the world keeps changing and will continue to do so long after a traditional exercise in financial planning is complete. Since traditional financial planning cannot take any of the "what ifs" into account, it is just not an adequate vehicle for enjoying your financial future.

"Needs-based" planning violates basic economic philosophy. At its core, economics is the study of how people allocate limited resources to satisfy unlimited wants. It is not a study of how particular things work in a vacuum. "Needs-based" planning focuses on one thing: the goal to have "X" dollars in "Y" years without regard to the living, changing world.

A financial plan that does not work under the greatest variety of circumstances is, in fact, no plan at all. When is the best time to start to do some real planning? The Chinese have a great expression; the best time to plant a shade tree was 25 years ago. If you did not do it then, the second best time is right now.

Part 4:
The Trouble With
Traditional Planning

In order for an individual investment to be sound, it must afford the owner safety, liquidity and control of the asset. "Safety" means that the investment does not engender an undue amount of risk. "Liquidity" means that the money is accessible. That is, you can get to the money without having to pay for the privilege of doing so. "Control" means that you can use the money any way you want and that you do not have to ask anyone else for permission to do so. The power of money is deeply minimized, or even rendered useless, unless you have all three. Let's discuss several investment vehicles and see how they measure up.

Uncle Sam Wants You ... To Have A 401(k) Plan

But do *you* want to have a 401(k) plan, an IRA, a defined benefit plan, a profit sharing plan or some other qualified plan? The most common investment vehicles that the government has created actually benefit the government considerably more than they benefit the affluent individual.

Consider this—by law, the federal government is not allowed to invest its income (your tax dollars) in the stock market. When you put money into a 401(k) or any other qualified plan, that money is, or can be, invested in the market. A big portion of your plan, in fact, belongs to the government. By depositing money into your qualified plan, the government circumvents this prohibition by having you invest in the stock market on its behalf—something that it is not legally allowed to do on its own.

If you have an IRA, a Keogh, a 401(k) plan or some other "qualified" plan, you contribute pre-tax dollars and you deduct the amount of those dollars from your taxable income in the year in which you make those contributions. A "qualified" plan is one that is "tax-qualified" under the tax code and is therefore tax-deferred. When you turn age fifty-nine and one-half, you are permitted to begin taking the money out of the plan without penalty. You must still pay ordinary income tax on every dollar you withdraw, but you do not have to pay any penalties.

Accountants and traditional financial planners favor these accounts because they reduce your tax bill in the short-term. However, qualified plans fail the safety, liquidity and control tests. They are illiquid because they do not allow you access to your money. Your control is highly limited as well. If a good opportunity comes along, you cannot use this money to take advantage of that opportunity unless you are willing to pay substantial penalties. So who controls the money? The government, not you!

Additionally, you cannot leverage the money in your qualified plan in any meaningful way. If you can borrow at all from your qualified plan, your right to do so is limited and there are stringent requirements with respect to repaying the money. Also, the interest that you pay to borrow from the plan is not tax-deductible and must be paid with after-tax dollars.

On the other hand, one of the best things about qualified plans is that they are liability proof. This means that if you get sued and lose, the plaintiff cannot take what is in your retirement account. This benefit is significant and illustrates why physicians love qualified plans even though there may be better ways of protecting their money.

In light of the litigious society in which we live, my physician clients are justifiably concerned about malpractice claims. Qualified plans appeal to those clients because of the creditor protection it affords them. As you will see however, there may be better ways to achieve the same level of protection without the significant drawbacks associated with qualified plans.

Qualified plans also serve as forced savings vehicles. The money invested in your plan can be withdrawn from your paycheck and invested directly into the plan before you ever get your hands on it. You never see that money, so you never get to take it to the mall. In our society this is a pretty important thing.

Most people who invest in qualified plans also claim that they "will be in a lower tax bracket" when they retire than they are in during their income earning years. If you subscribe to this theory, then this book is not for you. If being in a lower tax bracket is your goal, then I am not your guy and you should get advice from someone else. I want you to be in the maximum tax bracket when you retire because that would mean that you are living on more money! In any event, it is far more likely that if you are doing well now, you will be in the same high tax bracket, or in an even higher bracket, later on. So chances are, if you are putting money into a qualified plan today in a lower tax bracket, you will likely be taking it out later when you are in a higher tax bracket at a time when you probably have less tax deductions. When you look at it this way, qualified plans are hardly worthwhile!

Can you see why Uncle Sam is over in the corner licking his lips every time someone opens up a qualified plan?

Let's take a look at the very real and serious problems that come along with qualified plans.

1. The tax deferral is practically meaningless.

Many people are attracted to qualified plans because they can deduct their contributions from earned income and pay no income tax on the contributions in the year in which the contributions are made. They also pay no tax on the annual growth in their account. Yet, in many cases, taxpayers give back their entire tax savings in the first three years of their retirement.

Take the example of Samantha who puts $15,000 a year into a 401(k) plan from age thirty-five to age sixty-five. If we assume her marginal tax rate during that time period is thirty percent, she would have paid $4,500 in tax year each or a total of $135,000 over the course of those thirty years of investing. Now, if in retirement Samantha lives on an income of $250,000 pre-tax at an average tax rate of thirty percent, she will pay $75,000 a year in taxes. In short, Samantha will give back her entire tax savings—$135,000—in less than two years. After that, the government will continue to collect taxes on her savings (see Figure 4.1). Not only did Samantha, who followed all of the rules and did everything "right," fail to gain any tax benefits by socking all that money away in her 401(k) plan for thirty years, but she also gave up the use of that money during that period of time.

I often ask my clients, "If you had a farm, would you rather pay a tax on the seeds or the eventual harvest." The correct answer is that we would rather pay tax on the seeds. You can go to the garden store and buy a package of seeds for a few dollars. You can then plant those seeds and spend the next twenty-five years tending a garden that provides you with vegetables, fruits and great beauty—tangible and intangible benefits. Would you rather pay tax on a few dollars worth of seeds or on the hundreds of thousands of dollars of benefit that accrues to you over the life of that garden? Most people would rather pay a few dollars of tax on the seeds.

Figure 4.1

$15,000 at 30% = $4,500 of tax saved each year

$4,500 of tax saved each year for 30 years = $135,000 total tax saved

$250,000 retirement income at 30% tax rate = $75,000 of tax paid per year

$75,000 x 2 years = $150,000

$150,000 is greater than $135,000

---

2. The lower tax bracket argument.

What about the argument that you expect to be in a lower tax bracket at the time you retire? Most of my clients do not retire completely—they simply slow down. They work because they want to, not because they have to. They may work fewer hours, but generally they are making more income at age sixty or sixty-five than they did when they were putting money into their qualified plans decades earlier. They are also making more money from their assets then when they were working full time. There is no guarantee that you will be making less money and be in a lower tax bracket at retirement. And do you actually *want* to be?

Additionally, if you are like most people, you will have fewer tax deductions later in life. For one, if your house is paid off you would lose your mortgage interest deduction. Moreover, if you are lucky, your children will be out of the house and you will no longer be claiming them as dependents. Thus, not only will you be in the same tax bracket or a higher one, you will have fewer deductions to offset the amount of taxes that Uncle Sam wants.

There is also no guarantee that tax rates will stay the same. The government is always finding more and more ways to raise taxes, either in an obvious manner by shifting tax brackets higher, or in a subtler manner by taking away deductions and creating new fees. Just because you are in one particular tax bracket today does not mean that the same tax bracket will still exist by the time you retire. Running the country seems to get more and more expensive and the money to do so has to come from somewhere.

According to the Congressional Budget Office, in 1985, the average effective tax rate for top earners in the United States was twenty-seven percent.[1] The effective tax rate is the average tax that a taxpayer pays on every dollar that he or she earns. In 2007, the average effective tax rate for top earners in the United States was approximately thirty-one percent.[2] That represents more than a fourteen percent increase in effective taxation. So while it is true that the government has lowered the marginal tax brackets, the percentage of taxes that each taxpayer pays has actually increased because there are fewer deductions and because more things are taxed.

---

1.   Congressional Budget Office—"Effective Federal Tax Rates, 1979–1997", October 2001.
2.   Congressional Budget Office—"Effective Tax Rates Under Current Law, 2001 to 2014", August 2004.

Taxes are not going down and in truth, they really *cannot* go down. The government will need more money to operate in the future than it needs today. Every ten seconds starting at midnight on January 1, 2011 and continuing for the next eighteen years, a "baby boomer" will turn age sixty-five and expect Social Security. Where do you think that money is going to come from?

Social Security was first established as part of the New Deal—a social welfare program enacted during President Franklin Roosevelt's administration. At that time, there were approximately forty people working for every one person on Social Security. By the year 2011 there will only be two people working for every person receiving Social Security benefits. Additionally, as people live longer, they require more medical care and more long-term care. The government will pay for a significant portion of that care because a large segment of the population will be unable to afford it. Moreover, the war in which America is involved in the Middle East is expensive and there is no discernable end in sight. More recently, the government has spent a significant amount of money fighting terrorism and cleaning up natural disasters. Again, the money has to come from somewhere.

3. The money is taxable at ordinary income tax rates when you take it out.

When you get to fifty-nine and one-half years old, you are permitted to start withdrawing money from your qualified plan. Until that blissful day arrives, the qualified plan statement that you receive is a highly deceptive portrait of your financial condition. Keep in mind that a large percentage of the money in your qualified plan is going back to the government as taxes; only a portion of the funds in your qualified plan is yours. Yet people look at their qualified plan statement and say, "Woo hoo—I'm doing great!" In reality, *you* are doing just okay; it is the *government* that is really doing great.

When you make withdrawals from a qualified plan, those withdrawals are taxed at ordinary income tax rates, not at the considerably more favorable capital gains rates. So you lose again. And it gets worse. If a security you hold in your brokerage account results in a loss, you can write off that loss on your taxes. That is not true in the case of a qualified plan. The government figures that you are already getting a "tax deduction" (it is really a deferral), so why should they give you an additional benefit on top of that? This is why Uncle Sam gets to retire while the average American does not.

4. Total government control.

Do you really want the government to regulate what you do with your money? Consider that in most cases, you cannot take money out of a qualified plan without a penalty until you are age fifty-nine and one-half. Again, let's say that you are forty years old, there is $500,000 in your qualified plan and a great real estate deal or business opportunity comes along. You cannot get the money out of your plan without paying dearly for the privilege. As for taking out a loan from your qualified plan, do not even think about it!

One of the worst ways to borrow money is to borrow it from a retirement savings plan. First, you can only borrow a limited amount of the money. Yes, it is *your* money—but as long as it is locked up in "tax jail," the government has enormous control over what you can do with it. Second, you must pay back the money you borrow over a relatively short period of time. Third, the money you use to pay back the loan has already been taxed. This means that you use after tax dollars to pay off the loan only to have those same dollars taxed again when you withdraw them from the plan at retirement. Fourth, you receive no income tax deduction for the interest you pay on the loan. Fifth, there is a lost opportunity cost to taking money out of the plan—the money was not there growing for you while you had it out. Moreover, if you leave or lose your job, you must either repay the loan immediately or pay a tax and penalty on it.

As if all that is not bad enough, when you turn seventy and one-half years old, the government *compels* you to take the money *out* of the plan—you have escaped tax long enough and the government will apply a very significant penalty to your plan unless you begin withdrawing the money. In other words, you *have to* start taking the money out of the account or the government will take even more of it away. When you turn seventy and one-half, the government applies actuarial tables and requires you to remove at least a predetermined percentage of the value of the account called the "required minimum distribution" ("RMD"). Every year thereafter, the percentage goes up until you die. If you do not make those withdrawals, the government will be more than happy to charge you a fifty percent penalty on the money that you should have removed. If you die before it comes time to withdraw the money, you never get to use that money; consequently, the fact that you saved money in a place where you could not touch it for all those years is for naught. Qualified money that is not used correctly is not a good deal for anyone except, that is, the government.

Here is yet another problem. Not all that long ago, the government raised the age at which you can begin to receive Social Security benefits. What if the government changed the age of penalty-free withdrawals from qualified plans from the current age fifty-nine and one-half to sixty-five? This means that they could lock up your money until you are sixty-five! Yes, they can do this; they are the government after all! This would present a major problem for anyone planning to retire at age fifty-nine and one-half because they would have to wait an additional five and one-half years to access their money! Moreover, the government can also lower the age at which mandatory distributions must start. It is disturbing, but certainly not impossible.

5. Market Risk.

If you were unlucky enough to retire in 1999 with all of your qualified plan money invested in the stock market, by 2004, just five short years later, your net worth was probably body-slammed by the collapse of the NASDAQ and the general downturn in the stock market. What if the market drops again between now and when you retire, or after you have entered retirement? A qualified plan invested in the stock market carries an enormous amount of risk.

Additionally, most qualified plans offer limited investment choices. Typically, a qualified plan will offer the investor between six and fifteen choices. That relatively low number is not representative of the entire market. Why should you be limited to between six and fifteen options when there are so many other possibilities that might be better for you, if only you and your investment advisor knew about them?

Another negative aspect to these qualified plans is that they typically do not offer rebalancing. If one segment of your total investment strategy takes off, your portfolio will be out of balance. For example, if your large cap investments suddenly do very well, you will have a portfolio overly weighted toward large cap investments. Portfolio rebalancing means moving some of the money from the section of your portfolio that had some past success and reinvesting it in other segments. Rebalancing recognizes that the market is cyclical—what is up today may very well be down tomorrow. By failing to rebalance, you inadvertently place all of your eggs in the same basket, without control of that basket.

6. Qualified plans are not "self-completing."

"Self-completing" means that if, for any reason, you are unable to continue to fund the plan, the entity offering the plan will fund it for you. What if you become sick or injured or die? Do you think for a moment that Uncle Sam or the entity holding your 401(k) plan is going to step in and continue to make payments for you? Not in this lifetime.

7. No step up in basis at the date of death.

This is a little complicated, so stick with me on this one. Let's say that Fred, at age twenty-five, purchased $1,000 worth of stock in XYZ Corporation. By the time he died at age eighty, his XYZ stock was worth $1,000,000. If Fred held that stock outside of his qualified plan on the day he died, for tax purposes, the government would no longer consider the "basis" for that investment as the $1,000 he spent when he purchased the stock. The basis is the amount of money that the government uses as a measuring stick for determining what kind of gains take place from that point forward. Fred's stock would get a "stepped up" basis to the value it had on the day Fred died. Therefore, the stock would have a "basis" of $1,000,000.

In other words, with that "step up in basis," Fred's heirs now own an asset—$1,000,000 worth of stock—that they could sell the next day without having to pay any capital gains taxes. Without that step up in basis, Fred's heirs would have had to pay tax on the difference between the $1,000,000 that the stock is worth now and the $1,000 for which Fred bought it many years ago. A stepped up basis is an extremely valuable thing to one's heirs.

Qualified plans offer no step up in basis. If Fred had bought that stock through his qualified plan and it's value rose from $1,000 to $1,000,000, whether or not his heirs sold it the day following his death for $1,000,000, his heirs, absent using a stretch IRA which may ultimately just compound the pain (see section 8 below for a discussion of stretch IRAs), would be immediately liable for the income tax on the entire $1,000,000 because that money had never been taxed. They would also be liable for any estate tax due on that same money. That is a big chunk of change to hand over to Uncle Sam.

8. The estate taxes will kill you.

One big mistake people often make is not spending down the money in their qualified plans while they are alive. This could be the result of their fear of running out of money or the thought of having to pay income taxes on their withdrawals. This is a big mistake; after paying income tax and estate tax on the principal, it is quite possible that your heirs may be left with a mere fifteen percent of the original principal.

Let's take a look at what happens to a 401(k) plan or any
other qualified plan on the day that the owner of that plan
dies. Let's assume that there is $1,000,000 in the plan and it
is subject to both federal and state income tax. Of that
$1,000,000, as much as forty-five percent, or $450,000,
could be eaten up in federal and state income taxes. That
leaves about $550,000. Do the heirs get that money? Abso-
lutely not. Somewhere between forty-two and forty-five percent of the original amount—the entire million—may have
to be paid for estate taxes. There goes another $420,000 to
$450,000! The heirs could end up with as little as $100,000
to $130,000, while Uncle Sam and your state government get
$870,000 to $900,000! The best thing an affluent person can
do for their country is to die with a lot of money in their
qualified plan because the government will get almost all of
it, and the person's heirs will get merely dimes on the dollar.
In death, qualified plans are a terrible deal.

This example is an oversimplification of the tax issue; there
may be some state estate and state income taxes, and there
may be a credit for those taxes paid on the federal estate tax
return. Nevertheless, exclusively from a tax standpoint, a
qualified plan is clearly a tax nightmare.

The terms "applicable exclusion" or "unified credit" refer
to the amount of money that you can protect from being
subject to death tax. The problem is that at death, the applicable exclusion is usually taken up somewhere else in your
personal economic system, thus exposing your entire quali-

fied plan to estate tax if you die and income tax if you do not. Heads the government wins; tails the government wins.

Not to worry. The government has created a way for us to "improve" this situation—the "stretch IRA." When a beneficiary inherits an IRA, the beneficiary can elect to take the principal in the IRA and pay it down over their lifetime based on an actuarial formula provided in the tax code. However, a "stretch IRA" only compounds the taxation problem. A stretch IRA refers to the situation where John, who invested money in an IRA, dies and leaves his IRA to his son John Jr. The tax laws allow John Jr. to create a "stretch IRA"—to take the money from his father's IRA in what is essentially a second generation IRA. Any applicable estate tax must be paid at John's death. Then, John Jr. must take money out of that stretch IRA based on his actuarial life expectancy. The problem here is that John's money stays in "tax jail" even longer and the tax problem is further compounded. Remember, contrary to popular belief, the IRA does not grow "tax-free," it only grows tax-deferred. When John Jr. finally withdraws the money, he will be paying even more tax on his father's money.

9. Look out for the Success Tax!

Before the 1997 Taxpayer Relief Act, there was a "success tax" applied to people's qualified plans. Under the old law, when people were too successful in "saving for retirement," they were subject to a fifteen percent tax on their retirement funds. While this law is no longer in effect, it does not mean that the government will not bring it back if the people in Washington get hungry enough.

10. Some Good Stuff

At first glance, the employer match is probably the only good reason to put money into a qualified plan; but is it worth it? The employer match allows you to "get money for free" simply by contributing to your qualified plan. Employers will often match a percentage of an individual's plan contribution up to a small percentage of the employee's salary. Accordingly, in many cases it may make sense to contribute to your plan up to the extent of the match. Whether you decide to put money into a qualified plan in order to take advantage of an employer's match should be determined on a case-by-case basis after considering what else you can do with that money. Remember, you still cannot use your money or the match until you are fifty-nine and one-half years old without penalty, and when you do withdraw the money, it will be taxed at your ordinary income tax rate.

It is true that investing in a qualified plan is easy and painless since the money is deducted from your paycheck and you never run the risk of either frittering it away or spending it on necessities. This is called "forced savings," and forced savings can be a good idea for a lot of people. Yet there are many other ways to create a "forced savings" situation for yourself where there will be no temptation to spend money that you mark in advance for investment and retirement. You can create different forced savings situations in ways that have far fewer restrictions on the safety, liquidity and control of your money—the three hallmarks of a good investment.

One last reason people often site for putting money into a qualified plan is that they want to amass savings for their retirement. While this is a laudable goal, a qualified plan may not be the best strategy for saving for retirement. In short, for most individuals of means, pre-tax retirement savings plans are not all they are cracked-up to be. They will not get you where you want to go. That is, qualified plans will not get you any closer to your goal which is to have safety, liquidity and control now, and a great big pile of money down the road.

11. The Roths—not necessarily the best neighbors

Not too long ago, the government created the "Roth IRA" and more recently enacted the "Roth 401(k)." The way these plans work is that subject to government-instituted limitations, a person can put after-tax dollars into the Roths and have the money grow on a tax-free basis. When the government permits a person to take the money out of the plan, no tax is due on the money.

A Roth 401(k) or a Roth IRA may make sense if you are absolutely certain that you will be in a higher tax bracket when you retire than you are when you fund them. There are still severe restrictions on the use of that money. There are limitations on contributions to these plans, and you still pay taxes on the money going into the account. This is not quite analogous to sending your money to "tax jail." It is more like putting your money under house arrest with an ankle bracelet.

Fuggetaboudit

Even Tony Soprano would blush. A guy you have never met sidles up to you and says, "I want to be your business partner. I have a great idea that should get us about a ten percent rate of return per year. So, give me money every year for thirty-five years and I will hold it for us." He then tells you, "If you need the money back from me before the end of the thirty-five years, you will be charged a ten percent penalty plus a 'tax' equal to the rate that you pay on your personal income taxes to the government." He also informs you that "You will not have any access to your money, and if a better opportunity comes along, you will not be able to take your money out unless you pay me that penalty. And by the way," he says, "I am not going to put up any money of my own, but at the end of the thirty-five years, we will split all of the money that comes out of the investment—including the money that you put in." "Do we have a deal?" He asks with a big smile on his face.

This is not a Sopranos subplot; this is the way tax-qualified plans actually work. Accountants are hired to reduce your tax bill, and they certainly can get your tax bill down *this* year if you are willing to commit money to the kind of investment concept outlined above. This is why so many accountants routinely recommend that their clients put money into retirement plans and even maximize the possible contributions to those plans. But what is in it for you over the long term?

The current structure of tax-qualified retirement plans is of little use to the affluent individual. Just because it is a great deal for the government does not mean that it is a great deal for you.

Fuggetaboutit.

Is Your Money In Tax Jail?

Some qualified plans allow people to contribute as much as $250,000 per year. As such, many people tend to use their qualified plan as their answer to the question, "How should I invest all of my money?" People who put all of their money into their qualified plan often do so because everybody else "is doing it" and because they have read about qualified plans in the press. Again, just because others do it does not mean everyone should.

Unfortunately, many people assume that investing in a qualified plan is going to handle all of their retirement needs down the road. This is not true for a variety of reasons. There is a right way—and a wrong way—to use your qualified plan.

For most people, the right way to use a qualified plan is to use it as one investment vehicle among several and **not as the only vehicle**. This holds true even when all the money in your qualified plan is invested in a collection of mutual funds, and it is especially true when the money in qualified plans is invested entirely in one company's stock. There are several reasons why your qualified plan should be one of a variety of investment vehicles. First, you want to spread your risk among a variety of different investments and not keep all of your eggs in one basket. Think about the people who worked for Enron. Many Enron employees invested all of their 401(k) plan money in Enron stock and further received a match of Enron stock. When Enron tanked, not only did these hard-working, decent individuals lose their professional careers, they lost their life savings as well. Failing to balance risk among a variety of different investments amounts to financial suicide.

Will there be other Enrons? It is inevitable. Some companies will get into trouble because of dishonesty at the top—"crime in the suites," as the expression goes. Other companies will get into trouble, not necessarily through any fault of their own, but simply because market forces change things.

Take the airline industry. No one could have predicted 9/11 or the resulting impact it had on the airline industry. Similarly, no one could have predicted what the recent spike in oil prices has done to the industry either. Now, stable and respectable airlines such as United have gone hat-in-hand to the government, seeking bailouts and relief from obligations such as their commitments to pensions for their retired employees. It is bad enough that some United employees may not get their full pensions, but if United's stock was to plunge, what would happen to all of those United employees who had invested solely—or even primarily—in United stock?

It is impossible to predict the future. There are just too many variables that we cannot gauge. It is a certainty that some companies that have been highly successful for years, decades or even generations are going to fail. We do not know which companies are going to fail; consequently, we cannot predict whether your employer might be one of the casualties. Accordingly, it would be inadvisable to use your qualified plan as a "one size fits all" solution to the problem of how to invest for the future. Since we do not know what the future is going to hold, for ourselves or for individual companies, we should not—and cannot—take that much of a risk.

Another important reason to avoid using the qualified plan as the single solution to investment questions concerns the issue of liquidity. Liquidity refers to how quickly you can get your hands on your money if you want it or need it for any reason. A qualified plan, at least until you turn age fifty-nine and one-half, is about as illiquid an investment as you can imagine. Uncle Sam will make you jump through hoops to get your own money out of a qualified plan, and the cost of borrowing against your qualified plan or breaking that piggy bank and withdrawing the money is astonishingly high.

Assume that Dave, who has not read this book, is placing all of his investment dollars in his qualified plan. Suddenly he has an investment opportunity—a chance to buy a business, a piece of real estate or even a vacation home for his family. He has the money; but it is locked up in tax jail. Uncle Sam will not let him have it, at least not without paying a very steep price. Dave will not be able to take advantage of that other investment because his money is locked away. This is why it is so important to diversify your investment dollars among different assets. You never know what opportunities will arise down the road.

Also, contrary to popular belief, contributing money to your qualified plan does not put more money into your pocket today. In fact, another reason to be careful about making a qualified plan your primary investment tool is that it takes money *out* of your pocket today. You do not take home more money when you allocate pre-tax dollars to your qualified plan. Let's take the example of Ellen, a thirty-five year-old woman who earns $250,000 a year and allocates six percent of her income to her qualified plan. Ellen pays an average effective tax rate of thirty percent. If she did not take advantage of a qualified plan at all, she would pay $75,000 in tax on her earnings and she would have $175,000 in net (post-tax) income.

Since Ellen is allocating six percent of her income to her qualified plan, she is locking up $15,000 a year of her $250,000 in "tax jail." This leaves $235,000 of taxable income, and since she pays thirty percent in taxes, she has only $164,500 left over, compared with the $175,000 she would have had had she not invested in a qualified at all (see Figure 4.2). What could Ellen do with that extra $10,500? Certainly she could take a few trips, buy a flat screen TV, otherwise whittle the money away or invest that money in an investment tool that would earn her a far greater return.

For example, Ellen could take that $10,500 and put it in a tax-advantaged environment. She could invest it in tax-favored vehicles like municipal bonds, real estate or life insurance. She could even put the $10,500 in a money market account. Ellen may still come out ahead because she will have access to the money now. If she puts the money into the qualified plan, she will not see a dime of the money until she turns fifty-nine and one-half years old (if she lives that long). That is a long time for the government to deny Ellen access to her money, especially in a world where cash is king.

So how should you use your qualified plan? Make sure that you have other investments. When you retire, do not live off of the interest of that qualified plan. Instead, spend down your qualified plan first while your other investments, those that pass more estate tax efficiently, continue to grow.

"Spend it down" means "live on the money that the investment has created for you." The assets you want to spend down first are those that will not pass through your estate in a tax-efficient way. Certain types of assets are taxed very heavily when you die. Once you have gone through those heavily taxed assets, it will be time to utilize your other assets which will have had a longer time to grow. Assets outside of your qualified plan will pass in a more tax-advantaged way to your heirs than any money in your qualified plan would have.

This is the most efficient way to use your qualified plan. Do not think of your qualified plan as the solution to all of your investment decision-making, and do not fall into the trap of feeling virtuous and wise just because you have "maxed out" your qualified plan each year. Instead, spread your risk over a variety of investments and do not keep all of your eggs in one basket, especially if it is your employer's basket. Do not put any more money into "tax jail" than you have to, and when you turn fifty-nine and one-half years old, do not let your qualified plan keep growing into your seventies, eighties and nineties! You will be better off financially for making these choices … and so will those you love.

Figure 4.2

Without 401(k):

$250,000 taxable income x 30% rate = $75,000 tax paid

    $250,000 taxable income
    -$75,000 tax paid
    $175,000 take home after tax

With 401(k):

$250,000 x 6% = $15,000 to 401(k) plan
    $250,000 income
    -$15,000 401(k) contribution
    $235,000 taxable income

    $235,000 x 30% rate = $70,500 tax paid

    $235,000 taxable income
    -$70,500 tax paid
    $164,500 take home after tax

    $175,000 is greater than $164,500

Charity Begins At Home

Some investment advisors tell you that the smartest thing to do, if you have a lot of money locked up in a qualified plan, is to donate that money to charity. They claim that this will save you handsomely on taxes. While it is true that charitable donations save you money when it comes to taxes, it is equally true that your beneficiaries and heirs would rather have that money available to them. Saving the whales is a noble cause; however, your heirs may need that money more than the whales do!

I do not understand how a financial advisor can claim that he is giving you good "advice" when he tells you that the best way to save on taxes is to give your money away. After all, the idea of earning money is so that you can keep it, save it, spend it and give it to those you love. Don't get me wrong; I am completely in favor of charitable giving. However, we should give to charity because we *want* to—not to rectify an error we made by putting far too much money into a qualified plan or using it incorrectly in retirement.

Whether your objective is to give more money to charity or let your children inherit the money, there are ways to combine your qualified plan with other investment vehicles, such as life insurance and annuities, to substantially increase the amount of money that you pass on to either the charity or your children.

Tell Your Accountant No Thanks

You are a business owner and your accountant tells you that he has a great way for you to reduce your taxes this year. He tells you to create a profit sharing plan and to put $60,000 into it—$40,000 for you and $20,000 for your staff. Under this type of plan, you are required to give money to your employees' retirement accounts whether or not they participate. The accountant will look up from your paperwork with a smile and say, "I just saved you $25,000 in taxes!"

You just locked your money away in a qualified plan. In addition to the existing pitfalls of qualified plans, you have created another problem. If you had taken the $60,000 of income and paid tax on it, you would have had $30,000 to $40,000 of after-tax income to invest or spend as you see fit. Instead, you have a tax savings of $25,000, $20,000 of which you gave away to your employees! Financially, you may wind up with the same amount of dollars in an investment account, but now your money is under lock and key with the federal government and you gave away your tax deduction. Moreover, when you do take your money out, you will have the privilege of paying tax on it all over again (see Figure 4.3).

I understand that there may be good business reasons for a profit sharing plan, but there are less expensive alternatives for you as an employer. Additionally, rank and file employees often do not appreciate retirement plans because they have no access to the money until they retire, and in many cases, these employees have a real need for the money now.

Tell your accountant that instead of indulging in a short-term desire to minimize taxes, you want to do what makes the most sense in order to accomplish your real goal of being able to spend the most money you can while you are alive, and pass on the most money you can at death. Your accountant has noble motives—he or she is trying to save you money on your taxes *this* year. That is an accountant's job.

By way of contrast, it is my job to perform overall planning so that you can live on more money now and pass on more money later. That is why your accountant may not be the best source of guidance for you on this topic, especially if you are an individual with a high net worth.

Although there may be good business reasons to have a profit sharing plan (such as attracting and retaining good employees), there is no good long-term tax planning reason for the plan.

If you are going to be comfortable in retirement, it is essential to find a better financial balance between your retirement plan assets and the other financial vehicles you possess. You also need to have a financial strategy to help avoid or minimize the disadvantages of these retirement plans. Most people with qualified retirement plans have no exit strategy in place. They will therefore get hit with a large tax bill and have their wealth significantly eroded. What is worse, their beneficiaries can face both income and estate taxes on the plan assets. Your survivors may experience "tax shock" because the government will confiscate, in taxes, most of the assets of the plan that took you a lifetime to build.

Figure 4.3

With a Profit Sharing Plan:

As the employer, you contribute $60,000
    $40,000 goes to your plan
    $20,000 goes to your employees' plans

$40,000 per year at 6% for 30 years = $3,352,067

$3,352,067 x 40% tax rate = $1,340,827 tax due

      $3,352,067 value of account
      -$1,340,827 taxes
      $2,011,240 value of your account, net of taxes

Without Profit Sharing Plan:

$60,000 x 40% tax rate = $24,000

      $60,000 income to you
      -$24,000 taxes paid
      $36,000 to be invested

$36,000 per year growing at 5% (net of tax)* for 30 years = $2,511,388

SUMMARY
After tax value of Profit Sharing Plan = $2,011,240

After tax value of account without Profit Sharing Plan = $2,511,388

*Note that without the Profit Sharing Plan the account is non-qualified. Therefore it is taxable and not tax-deferred. It could be invested in a vehicle incurring no taxes such as Municipal Bonds. It could also be invested in a place where it gets capital gains treatment. That is why the non-qualified account grew at five percent and the qualified account grew at six percent.

Don't Tax You, Don't Tax Me ...

Senator Fritz Hollings had a colorful expression for the philosophy of Congress when it came to taxation. It boiled down to this: "Don't tax you, don't tax me. Tax the fella behind that tree."

In other words, somebody is going to pay a big tax bill, and that "somebody" is whoever has the least amount of clout in Washington. While it is true that President George W. Bush has *technically* kept his promise to lower tax brackets, in reality, he has done anything but. Allow me to explain.

You may be familiar with the Alternate Minimum Tax ("AMT"). The AMT resulted from a tax law passed in 1969. It is a tax device that was designed to make sure that just about everybody who makes a relatively substantial amount of money has to pay some tax. It was meant to crack down on wealthy tax dodgers but instead has become the bane of the middle class. In 1970, approximately 20,000 taxpayers were subject to the AMT.[3] In its 2004 Annual Report to Congress, the National Taxpayer Advocate estimated that approximately 3,500,000 taxpayers were affected by the AMT in 2006.[4] That number is expected to grow to 34,800,000 by the year 2010 if the law is not changed.[5] The AMT falls most

---

3.   Greg Leiseron and Jeff Rollay; Tax Policy Center—"Individual Alternative Minimum Tax", November 10, 2006.
4.   Nina E. Olson; "National Taxpayer Advocate Report to Congress", January 2004.
5.   Nina E. Olson; "National Taxpayer Advocate Report to Congress", January 2004.

heavily on the upper middle class—those individuals who earn more than $150,000 each year. While President George W. Bush *did* lower the top marginal tax bracket from thirty-six percent all the way down to thirty-five percent (how can we ever thank you?), he applied a little sleight of hand in order to make sure that the government continued to rake in even more money. That sleight of hand came about by failing to adjust for inflation the income level that triggers the Alternate Minimum Tax. What the government gave you with one hand, it took back—and more—with the other.

This is especially true if you are among the top wage earners in the country. While you would think that you would pay slightly less in income tax as a result of that miniscule reduction in the top income tax bracket, you are actually paying more. This is because people seem to trigger the AMT at lower and lower income levels. Right now, for most people, the income level that triggers the AMT hovers around the $150,000 mark. The AMT is a tax—a hidden tax—that falls disproportionately and unjustly on those who make a significant amount of money.

Keep in mind that Congress' failure here is not that they passed this law recently. Instead, their failure is that they have never changed the law or indexed it for inflation. When the AMT was passed years ago, only wealthy people were affected by it. As inflation mounted, the AMT reached further and further down the socioeconomic levels of our society to the people who are essentially the middle class earners. Why hasn't the government rectified this? Because it makes them money! The more people subject to the AMT, the more money there is flowing to Washington.

This AMT issue is partly responsible for the fact that in 1985, the average effective tax rate for the highest income earners in the United States was lower than it is today.[6] So, while it is true that the government has lowered the marginal tax brackets, the percentage of taxes that each taxpayer pays has actually increased because there are fewer deductions and because additional things are taxed.

Do not hold your breath waiting for taxes to go down any time soon. Your only recourse is to write your Congressperson to seek relief—and this is hardly an effective solution to a vexing problem.

Lost Opportunity Costs

"Opportunity cost" is a term economists use to measure what you could have done with a particular pool of money. Any time that you make a financial decision, you necessarily decide not to do other things with that money. For example, if you spend $5,000 on that spur-of-the-moment getaway, you have incurred a measurable lost opportunity cost in that the $5,000 is no longer available for your use.

---

6. Congressional Budget Office—"Effective Federal Tax Rates, 1979-1997", October 2001. Congressional Budget Office—"Effective Tax Rates Under Current Law, 2001 to 2014", August 2004.

Suppose I went out into the street and threw a one-dollar bill into the wind, never to see it again. My loss was not just the one-dollar bill that I discarded. The true economic loss was that dollar plus everything that that dollar could have earned over time.

We can determine the lost opportunity cost of any economic decision by determining what that money would have grown to had it been invested in your best investment in your individual economic system. For example, assume that when you invest money in your best investment, your average rate of return is eight percent after taxes. In this scenario, had you invested the $5,000 in the eight percent investment, at the end of thirty years your $5,000 would have grown to a future value of $50,314.

Of course, this analysis does not mean that you should never go on vacation again. It simply illustrates that there was an economic cost to the vacation that exceeded the pure dollar amount that you spent on it. It should also be pointed out that there were probably beautiful memories that you gained from the vacation that cannot be measured monetarily. I do not mean to say that you should not enjoy your money. On the contrary, you should absolutely trade your dollars for great memorable experiences.

Why is lost opportunity cost important to financial planning? The answer is clear: if we can examine why certain decisions or strategies are inefficient and we can improve their efficiency, then we can create more wealth without it costing us more money.

Compounding The Pain

When you keep too much money in a liquid environment like a savings account or a money management account, you generally lose money due to inflation and taxes. Let's see how this works. Suppose you leave money in a savings account or an interest-bearing checking account paying four percent interest per year. After taxes your net return is about two percent per year. Unfortunately, inflation rises at a rate of three percent per year these days. That means that you are not making four percent on your money. You are actually losing one percent after inflation and taxes.

The loss, however, is considerably greater than that. What if that same money was invested differently and received a net return of six percent interest per year? Instead of being down one percent to inflation, you could actually be ahead of inflation by three percent. So, what could you have done with that six percent on your money? You could have done a lot! Once you create a positive return on your money, the money you have earned can go out there and work just as hard for you. Albert Einstein said that the greatest force in the universe was the compounding of numbers. In the financial world, this could not be more true as long as the compounding is done in an efficient manner.

The Magic Mountain

A mutual fund is an actively managed collection of securities overseen by a "fund manager." The fund manager's goal is to keep the net asset value ("NAV") of the fund, as reported in the Wall Street Journal, or any other financial magazine or newspaper, as high as possible. The fund manager's goal is not to make you the most money. It is to keep the NAV as high as possible. So, that manager may very well do things that are not advantageous to you as an individual investor. If the fund manager sells holdings within one year of having purchased them, you—not the fund—will be paying tax at your marginal ordinary income tax bracket on the gain from that sale. Had you controlled the investment, you might have held on to those securities for at least a year in order to get long term capital gains treatment. That, however, is not the fund manager's concern since the manager is seeking to maximize the NAV, and the manager is not worried about your tax bill this year.

A mutual fund manager might also find it necessary to sell securities in order to liquidate a part of the portfolio so that other people can get their money out of the fund upon redemption. This too poses a problem for you because you will receive a tax bill for gains that you have not yet realized. Even though you might not have owned the mutual fund when the fund originally purchased those securities, upon their sale you will receive a Form 1099 and be required to pay a tax as a result of the sale executed by the fund manager.

Your shares in the fund may even go down in price as a result of the sale, but you will still owe a tax at the end of the year.

In baseball, if you are a relief pitcher and you enter into a game with men in scoring position, your personal earned run average or "ERA" is not charged if those men score. That is fair because *you* did not put the men on base. The reverse is true in the mutual fund world. When you buy into a mutual fund, you buy into other peoples' gains and losses. Inherently, there are gains and losses embedded in the fund and you will be responsible for them if the fund manager liquidates securities, for whatever reason. You have no say in the matter. Clearly, they are not playing baseball on Wall Street.

In addition, when you own shares in a mutual fund, you are responsible for the fees and trading costs that may be in excess of the management fee you are paying. Trading costs are transactional costs incurred by the fund to buy and sell different securities. These costs are passed on to the people who own shares of the fund. It may be difficult or even impossible to find these fees and costs spelled out in the fund's prospectus. They nevertheless exist and they cut into your gain and carry a lost opportunity cost into the future.

Those beautiful graphs that you see in mutual fund advertisements, where the amount of money that the fund earns just keeps going up, look a lot like an artist's rendition of a mountain. The peak gets higher and higher until it is lost in the clouds. The reality is that no investment grows as quickly and lavishly as those mountain pictures in the mutual fund ads. The mutual fund advertisements never show you that there are taxes and fees that you will have to pay on the income the fund has earned. The taxes and fees eat into that beautiful mountain and lead to lost opportunity costs. That money cannot be invested and must go to the government or the mutual fund company. Those charts are very misleading. The mountains only look magical due to the hype created by the advertising agency for the mutual fund. In fact, what you do not see in those mutual fund ads are the icebergs made up of taxes and lost opportunity costs that exist below the surface of the chart that slow down the rate of growth of your investment.

Individual Stocks ...

You should not trade individual stocks unless you have the time, patience and expertise to monitor and rebalance your portfolio. Additionally, you should only trade stocks if you do not mind paying the transaction costs to buy and sell securities. Most people who invest in individual securities tend to dabble in the market and "churn" through a lot of positions, taking profits and losses along the way (generally more losses than profits). Or the opposite will happen—they will buy securities and become distracted by other parts of their life and fail to spend the time necessary to keep their portfolios in a constant state of balance. If either of these scenarios sounds familiar, you may want to think twice before investing in individual securities.

Individual securities also carry a formidable amount of risk for the average investor. It is doubtful that Enron or Bear Stearns will be the last stocks to tank! Most people's crystal balls are pretty cloudy, so we cannot tell exactly which successful, respected "Fortune 500" company is headed for disaster. Yet it is undeniable that some of them are. Big companies are more at risk than ever before. Technology is changing rapidly. The political situation in the world changes daily. Competition from foreign companies has never been more intense and is only likely to grow. It is hard to think of a single blue-chip stock that could not be threatened by the ever-changing reality of today's world.

It used to be true a generation or two ago, that a healthy portfolio might contain 1,000 shares of IBM and 5,000 shares of AT&T. Today, betting a substantial portion of one's net worth on a single company, no matter how respected that company might be, is a recipe for disaster. Think about people who had money in Enron, Global Crossing, WorldCom or any other stock that went from high value to wallpaper almost overnight.

In order to be adequately diversified, an individual stockholder must have a significant amount of money in his portfolio. The stockholder must constantly rebalance his portfolio so that the portfolio does not become too heavily weighted toward any individual security or market sector. The downside to that rebalancing is that there will be trading costs and taxes associated with the buying and selling of the securities, and it takes a tremendous amount of time and effort. The trading costs may also be elevated if small amounts of a security—odd lots—may need to be sold or purchased rather than large blocks.

It is a simple fact that people do not get rich investing their own money in the market. Even Warren Buffet made his billions with the use of other people's money. Buying individual stocks is unwise because the risk of something happening to any one company is far too great. The best way to invest in securities is either with the aid of a professional, who has more access to information than the average person reading the Wall Street Journal or by diversifying your money in separately managed accounts or in several different mutual funds.

Whenever you go into a situation on your own, the prospects for taking a huge hit are always present. After all, you are up against experts who have far greater access to market-moving information than you do. There is almost no way that the individual investor can succeed with individual stocks. It is a game only for the super wealthy or for people who are willing to shoulder far too much risk with their investment dollars.

A better way for the affluent investor to invest in individual securities is to do so through what most people call "separately managed accounts." Separately managed accounts are market-based accounts where an investor selects a particular market allocation. The investor, usually with the help of a financial professional, selects what percentage of his portfolio he would like to invest in a number of different sectors. The account can include stocks, bonds, real estate investment trusts (REIT's) and international securities. Each sector then becomes a separately managed account.

The company that hosts the separately managed accounts typically keeps statistics on money managers. The company then goes out and hires who it believes to be the best performer or manager in each of the sectors that it offers—an "all-star" at every position. Each manager is offered a short-term contract and is required to stay within his or her discipline. That way, the bond guy is not managing small cap stocks. Using our baseball analogy, this means that the short stop is not pitching. This also insures that the portfolio does not overlap. In separately managed accounts, the managers are separated by market sector and therefore cannot buy the same securities; contrast this to mutual funds in which the risk of overlap is high.

The true beauty of separately managed accounts is that rebalancing happens on a non-emotional and consistent basis. Whenever one sector becomes unbalanced with respect to the rest of the portfolio, that sector is either bought or sold to bring the portfolio back into balance. This forces people to buy low and sell high rather than rely on last year's winner. For example, suppose large cap growth had a great quarter and that portion of your portfolio was up ten percent while the rest of your portfolio was flat. Your overall portfolio allocation would dictate that you lock in your gains and sell some of your large cap growth portfolio and buy securities that were relatively depressed.

Using separately managed accounts may also allow you to do what is commonly referred to as "tax loss harvesting." This means that you can limit your short-term capital gains—which are taxed at higher rates than long-term gains—by realizing your potential losses to offset those gains. This technique does not make up for the loss, but it can help lessen any tax "bite" that you would otherwise have to pay. For instance, the loss that you incur when you sell ABC stock might be used to reduce the capital gains liability generated by the sale of XYZ stock.

Additionally, in some separately managed accounts, you can typically avoid the trading costs associated with mutual funds. Also, many separately managed accounts are tax-managed and can be tailored to your particular tax situation. Remember, the more money you keep, the more growth you get. Many separately managed account programs also give investors the opportunity to do socially conscious investing. Thus, if you would like some market exposure, a separately managed account program is a much more sophisticated and efficient way to do it.

Hedging Your Bets

Chances are, if you have been to a cocktail party where people talk about investments, someone in your circle has invested money in a hedge fund. Hedge funds are typically organized as limited partnerships or limited liability companies. The hedge fund manager is the general partner or manager and the investors are the limited partners or members. In a hedge fund, the investors' money is pooled together and the general partner or manager serves as the "unconstrained" investment decision-maker for the fund.

In return for managing the fund, the hedge fund manager receives both a management fee and a performance incentive fee. The management fee, which varies from fund to fund, is a percentage of the assets under management and is typically about two percent of the fund's assets. The incentive fee, which also varies from fund to fund, is usually twenty percent of the profit of the fund.

Hedge funds are receiving a lot of attention these days. They are popular because people want an alternative to a traditional stock market investment that actually gives them the possibility of making some real money. The problem is that the only person that is guaranteed to do well in a hedge fund, no matter what, is the manager of the hedge fund. It is a high risk, minimally regulated, private investment fund that is usually characterized by "unconventional strategies." It is not for the faint of heart. Accordingly, the decision to invest in a hedge fund must be based on research and knowledge. Unfortunately, many high net worth individuals are jumping head first into hedge funds without having done their homework.

The more homework you do on hedge funds, the more likely it is that you will come to the conclusion that it is a game only for the mega wealthy. If you have a seven to eight figure net worth or more and you can afford to lose the $250,000 that it generally takes to get started as an investor in a hedge fund, go right ahead. It comes back to that basic principle that I described earlier: do not allow greed to dominate your portfolio, but allow greed an appropriate place *in* your portfolio. If you have millions and you can afford to risk—and lose—millions, then hedge funds may be appropriate for you.

Let me tell you about a situation that occurred in my office. A couple, Tom and Francesca, came to me to ask my advice about investing in a hedge fund. Tom is a hardworking business owner who had $400,000 in his qualified plan. Francesca, a city manager, had $230,000 in her qualified plan. Tom's best friend, Max, is one of those extremely rare individuals with the ability to pick individual stocks in the market, and Max started a hedge fund.

Tom and Francesca wanted in.

I asked why.

"We want to invest in the hedge fund," Tom said, "because Max has always done really well in the market. We want to get a piece of that."

I had to be the bad guy. I told them that since their entire portfolio amounts to $630,000, they simply cannot take $250,000—almost forty percent of it—and bet it on any one risky investment, no matter how strong the track record or no matter how close the relationship. I also told them that I do not think it is wise for people to invest such a high percentage of their means in a potentially risky venture.

"But the fund was up twenty percent last year!" Francesca argued. "And Max is Tom's best friend!"

I reminded them that many hedge funds have been up twenty percent in years when the market was strong. But, in other years, many of them have been down just as much. The only person who definitely makes money on a hedge fund is the person who runs the hedge fund.

Moreover, hedge funds are not all that interested in smaller investors, just as small investors should not be interested in hedge funds. A hedge fund is limited to 499 limited partners or members. Once the fund has 500 investors it has to comply with many more governmental regulations including reporting and investment requirements. Thus, hedge fund managers only want mega-millionaires and other highly wealthy people in the fund so that they can gather assets without exceeding the 499-person limit.

If you want to invest in a hedge fund, I advise you to refrain from using the hedge fund as an overly large part of your portfolio. And certainly, do not hedge your bets with a hedge fund if you do not have money to burn.

The End Is Near

Think back to the year 2000. You go into a deli for a roast beef sandwich. As the deli owner is making the sandwich, what is he watching on TV out of the corner of his eye?

Back in 2000, he was watching the NASDAQ ticker. That is because he had taken all of the savings he had accumulated from twenty years of owning and working in the deli business and bet them on tech stocks.

Go back to that same deli today. The deli owner is still there, making roast beef sandwiches, because he lost the paper profits he made when the tech bubble burst. Now, what is he watching out of the corner of his eye as he makes your sandwich? That's right—he is watching what is happening with interest rates because he took all of the savings he made in the five years since he got wiped out after the tech bubble and put them all into real estate.

When the deli owner or some other non-financial professional is getting deeply into one form of investing or another, you can count on the fact that the shrewd investors have already taken their money off the table. The easiest way to predict the collapse of one sector of the market is to see that a lot of people who have no business being in that investment have staked everything they own on getting rich that way.

In fact, as proof that the average person does not know what they are doing with respect to the market, a counterintuitive investment theory called the "Odd Lot Theory" was developed. An odd lot investor is a personal investor who trades stocks in less than one hundred share increments. The odd lot theory investment strategy is based on the belief that these small investors are guilty of bad timing and that profits can be made by acting contrary to odd-lot patterns.

Clearly, greed is the undoing of the middle class. Whether it was in gas stocks in the eighties, tech stocks in the nineties or real estate in this first decade of the new millennium, it is always the same. Everybody goes out and bets a lot of money in an area they know little or nothing about, simply because they heard about somebody else getting rich doing the same thing the day before.

The moral of the story: do not let greed drive the bus.

Saving For College

Today, parents are made to feel guilty if they are not socking away some dough for their children's college education. A variety of new savings vehicles are coming into existence specifically created to help people save for college. In almost every case, these new investment vehicles are not the most "sound economic investments."

Saving for college is a decision primarily based on emotions and not on logic. A 529 educational savings plan, or any vehicle that exists for the purpose of saving money for one particular expense, employs what essentially amounts to a "save and spend" strategy. Save now, spend later, when the tuition bills come due.

But "save and spend strategies" are almost inevitably doomed to fail because they are inherently economically unsound. Here is why. In the case of most investments, the initial years offer flat growth curves. It is not until the later years of the investment that the slope of the curve rises and becomes steep. The "save and spend" approach means that you sock away money which does not really get to grow significantly because you are forced to liquidate that account and spend it before you reach the steep part of the investment curve. In other words, the money that you get out is really a repayment of what you put in. Chances are, there was not enough time to allow your money to really work for you (see Figure 4.4).

From an economic standpoint, it would be wiser to borrow the money for tuition bills as they come due and repay those loans later with the money your investments make during the steep growth years. As long as you are investing money wisely, you do not need to think about breaking out a portion of your investments and dedicating them to college tuition. "Save and spend" takes away your opportunity to maximize the returns on your investments. In fact, it may be better to borrow money than sell off your investments before they start to become truly lucrative. And, depending on where you borrow the money from, you may be able to create a tax deduction simply by sending your child to college. For instance, you can create such a deduction if you use a home equity loan or a mortgage to pay for college.

Remember, you can borrow money for college, but you cannot borrow money for retirement. Moreover, the laws giving 529 plans or any other college savings vehicles special treatment may change at any time, which means that you, and your hard-earned investment dollars, are subject to the whim of Congress. College plans are designed to do only one thing—invest money for one specific purpose. Therefore, by investing in college savings plans you are not maximizing the effectiveness of the money you lock away. Keep in mind that when you sock away money in this sort of plan, you create enormous lost opportunity costs. If you become disabled or die, the plan is not "self-completing"—there is no automatic mechanism for completing the investment necessary to pay for your child's education. Most college savings plans are also subject to market risk. It is nice to project that the market will go up by "X" percent a year, but it can go down by just as much!

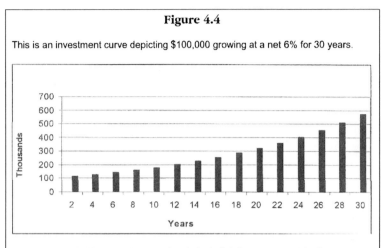

Figure 4.4

This is an investment curve depicting $100,000 growing at a net 6% for 30 years.

Note that from 0–18 years, the curve is relatively flat. If you were to take the money out of the investment after 18 years, you would lose the growth on the steep part of the curve and have to start all over again at the beginning (or flat part) of the curve.

If You Must Save For College

Despite the economic pitfalls, if you still feel the need to put money into a college plan, I would recommend the 529 plans. Under the current law, when money is taken out of a 529 plan to pay for higher education, it comes out tax-free and you can change the beneficiary to any "eligible family member" of the original beneficiary without penalty. An "eligible family member" is almost any person as far removed as a first cousin of the original beneficiary. That means that if your oldest child receives a scholarship, you can shift the money to your second child. If you withdraw the money for any reason other than college, you must pay a ten percent penalty and ordinary income tax on the gain in the account.

You would have, however, still obtained tax-deferred growth on the account for all of the years that the money was in the plan prior to withdrawing it.

Confession time: despite the fact that I am not in love with any form of college savings plan, I have three 529 plans myself. I have three children and emotionally I know that at the end of the day, I have put some money away for college tuitions. This way if something bad happens funding college educations is one less thing that my family needs to worry about. I do not, however, fully fund the plans. In fact, I contribute the *minimum* amount of money that I have to put in to avoid account fees. The plans also act as a good holding tank for gifts and birthday money that my children receive.

As we have seen, the "save and spend approach," which is the basis of the 529 plan, the Coverdale plan, the Education IRA and all other college savings vehicles, is simply not the wisest way to invest money. There is, however, an even *less* wise savings vehicle: the Uniform Gift to Minors Account (UGMA). This is an account to which your child has immediate access simply by turning the age of majority in your state. Your children do not have to go to college, and there is nothing you can do about keeping them from the money if it has been set-aside in such an account. Not all eighteen or even twenty-one year-olds are capable of making wise financial decisions. (Were you?) When we put money aside for our children's education, we feel good about ourselves. However, as I have shown, the problem is that children often get big before they get smart.

Some people use the UGMA because they assume that small children are in a lower tax bracket than they are themselves. This is not true. According to the law, your children under the age of fourteen share the same high tax bracket that you do. This may give them some interesting bragging rights in pre-school or even elementary school, but it does nothing for you from an investment standpoint. Essentially, if you are depositing money into a fund for your children, it is not quite tax jail; it is more of a "tax time-out."

We are not doing our children a favor giving them the option of either going to Harvard or buying a Harley, or going to Columbia verses buying a Corvette. Most eighteen year-olds cannot handle large sums of money. The overwhelming majority can barely handle any money at all—that is, unless they have gone out and actually earned it. The last thing any parent wants to see is his or her child in an airport, selling flowers for some offbeat religious group. Those groups are out there, and they are looking for kids, especially kids with money. Do not let your hard-earned money end up in the pocket of some brainwashing guru.

Term Insurance

Since there is less than a two percent chance that a term life insurance policy will pay a death benefit, there is a significant lost opportunity cost associated with term life insurance.[7] Forty-nine out of fifty times, the insurance company gets to keep all of the money it collects from you, Mr. or Ms. Term Life Insurance Buyer. If you had invested the term life insurance premiums elsewhere, chances are, your alternative investment would have had a positive rate of return. Thus, there is a tremendous lost opportunity cost associated with term life insurance ninety-eight percent of the time.

Let's take the example of Bob, a forty-five year-old man who carries $5,000,000 worth of term life insurance. He has five separate policies for $1,000,000 each, and each policy has an annual premium of about $1,500. Ten times a year, Bob writes a check for $750 to cover the semi-annual premiums on those policies. This amounts to $7,500 a year. Bob does not notice that $7,500 of his hard-earned, after-tax dollars are leaking away because he is writing checks in $750 increments.

Let's take a look at the lost opportunity cost that Bob creates. You can go to my website or the Internet and find what is called a "future value calculator." This is a financial tool that allows you to measure how much an asset is likely to grow in value over a given period of time. In Bob's case, if he keeps the term life insurance for twenty years, until he is age sixty-five, his annual payment of $7,500 a year over twenty years would have totaled $150,000 of money spent—for which there is no return, unless, unfortunately, Bob dies

---

7.   Penn State University, "1993 Study on the Fate of Term Insurance Policy".

before he turns age sixty-five. Is Bob's loss limited to that $150,000? Absolutely not.

If Bob were able to earn a six percent after-tax rate of return on the $7,500 per year that he is currently spending on term life insurance, at age sixty-five, Bob would have an asset worth $292,445. That is a significant amount of money to forgo.

This certainly does not mean that Bob should not have any life insurance. He absolutely should. After all there is a risk (albeit a small one) that he will die prematurely, and if that happened, his family would undoubtedly suffer a tremendous financial loss in addition to the emotional one. Although term insurance is not the most economical life insurance, it is far better than no life insurance at all. The challenge is finding a way to provide the death benefit more efficiently and eliminate Bob's loss of the $292,445.

Part 5:
Characteristics Of A Great Plan

As you have already read (and will read again), traditional financial planning does not work. Instead, people must achieve financial balance in their lives. The only way you can do this is by establishing a "comprehensive, economically efficient system." A "comprehensive, economically efficient system" creates economic certainty and affords you peace of mind. It is comprehensive in that it takes into account all of the factors affecting you and your family's economic life internally and from the outside world. It is efficient and systematic in that it is flexible enough to change when necessary, and it is easy and inexpensive to create, use and track. It must also work despite the fluctuation in the stock market or changes in the tax rates or laws.

Financial Portfolio Versus Investment Portfolio

When people think of financial planning, they generally think of the term "asset allocation." Asset allocation means looking at your portfolio and seeing if you have an appropriate ratio of stocks to bonds, large cap versus small cap stocks, value versus growth companies and domestic versus international investments. Most financial planners have predetermined ratios of what they consider appropriate levels of asset allocation. Accordingly, they tend to plug all of their clients into the same basic asset allocation models.

The problem is that when it comes to financial planning, one size does not fit all. There is no one magic approach; there is no single set of perfect numbers or one "golden mean" that suits everyone. We all have different time frames, different amounts of money to work with, different levels of risk tolerance and different levels of expertise. When financial planners focus exclusively on asset allocation, they overlook the big picture. The big picture does not involve questions of large cap verses small cap stocks, but whether you should have any stocks or mutual funds at all. Instead of focusing on the allocation of assets within your qualified plan, you must first answer the real question of whether you should have a qualified plan in the first place.

I call these sorts of questions *true macroeconomic questions*, which is a fancy way of saying the "big picture." If your investment advisor is simply trying to figure out where to stick your money instead of looking at the big picture, you have a problem. When I work with my clients, we start with a macroeconomic analysis of what is going on in their entire financial world, and we discuss what they would like to accomplish in their financial lives. This means that we consider all the products they currently own and all of the products that are available to them, some of which they may not even know exist. Then we figure out what fits and what does not fit.

Most financial planners do not realize that car insurance, home insurance, wills and trusts are in fact things that affect your financial life. Few financial planners take a holistic view of their clients' financial lives. They are too busy using cookie cutter formulas for asset allocation instead of trying to determine what a client really needs or wants. Again, there is no magic product out there. It is having a unique, personalized strategy that makes people successful. First figure out your goals, and then come up with a strategy to develop financial balance implementing products that will most quickly and efficiently enable you to meet and exceed those goals.

There Is No Such Thing As A Bad Investment

There is no such thing as a good investment either. No one investment is good or bad in and of itself. However, some investments are sold to people improperly, either by those who do not know better or by boiler room operations that have no regard for their financial well-being. Before buying a product, one must ask the question: does this particular investment fit well with the rest of my financial life?

Financial planners are akin to pharmacists because investments are like prescription drugs. Pharmacists must be very careful to monitor the interactions of the various medications prescribed to an individual. Guarding your financial health is no different; you do not want to have strategies that conflict with each other. Accordingly, you have to take the time to figure out whether your financial planner is looking out for your best interests, and if not, you must find a better guardian for your financial health.

Sometimes we hear the phrases "macroeconomic" and "microeconomic" analysis, and it sounds a little overwhelming or frightening. Put simply, economics is "the science which studies human behavior as a relationship between ends and scarce means which have alternative uses."[1] The way to get the most out of your personal economic system is to make sure that all your resources are being used efficiently.

The most efficient way to use your money is to have it working for you in multiple ways at the same time. You can talk on the phone, check your email, glance at the TV and prepare a meal all at the same time. Traditional financial planning does not know how to make your money "multitask." Instead, traditional financial planning compartmentalizes your money. It puts some of your money into one financial product for retirement, another for college, yet a third for estate planning and so on. You can multitask, so why shouldn't your money?

---

1.   Robbins, Lionel. *An Essay on the Nature and Significance of Economic Science.* London; Macmillan and Co., Limited (1945).

Compartmentalization of money and separating dollars for different needs, are some of the basic reasons why traditional financial planning is inefficient and therefore subject to failure. This is true even for the many people who take the time to think through their financial lives. Money needs to multitask in order to work efficiently; it is possible to have the same dollar performing many functions.

What makes a master chess player great? In an article written by Les McGuire, MBA, dated August 19, 2003, McGuire suggests that it is not his ability to predict the future. Instead, he says that it is the chess player's talent for making "moves that leave him in an ideal position, both in terms of safety and opportunity," regardless of the moves made by his opponent. The game of chess is not won by focusing on the power of a particular piece. Instead, McGuire states that the successful chess player wins because he successfully coordinates the power of those pieces over the course of the entire game. The lowly pawn may ultimately make the queen more powerful. Master chess players value protecting their pieces above opportunity; they know that if they avoid losing resources, they will ultimately gain more opportunity. You should establish that same approach to ensure the financial success of your life. You should not look down the road trying to predict the future; instead, you should ask yourself how you can place yourself in the most efficient and advantageous position at all times.

Your most advantageous position is to develop strategies that first protect your assets and then second, make your assets work and grow more efficiently. When speaking of protection, I mean that your strategies must protect you from wealth-eroding factors such as taxes, inflation, liability, disability, death and market risk. After you and your assets are protected, the strategies must then achieve efficiency and growth. This means that you must pay lower taxes, take less risk, have more flexibility and control your assets while living on more money and passing more money to your heirs. It may seem hard to believe, and it probably runs counter to what typical financial planners may tell you, but more money slips through your fingers because it is eroded by risk, inflation and taxes than by picking the wrong investments. It is much more important to protect your wealth and use great strategies to create more of it, than it is to seek investments that may possibly give you an additional one or two percent of growth with considerably more risk.

Nevertheless, financial institutions tell you over and over, that in order to get more return, you must take more risk. This is simply not true. When you combine proper and efficient strategies, you can achieve greater rates of return with no additional risk.

I am advocating a shift to financial balance where the emphasis is on "strategy, not product." There is no one individual financial product that is right for everybody, no one magic bullet. If there was, everybody would invest in that one thing, and life would be simple. Unfortunately, that is not how things work. You need an advisor who has the best possible strategies for you, not an advisor who claims that he or she has the best possible product. Product-based advisors often choose products on the basis of the fees they receive for selling those products. Does this sound like they have your best interests at heart?

Buying a new driver will not improve your golf swing any more than buying a new financial product will improve your overall financial outlook. The idea of making millions by finding and buying the right investment is about as likely as financing your retirement with lottery tickets. Think about all of the financial planning and financial products that are available in the marketplace today. Yet, how is the average American really doing? Personal debt, bankruptcies and foreclosures are at an all-time high and growing, despite the fact that the economy has been relatively strong for more than a dozen years. Banks and investment companies are no different from golf club manufacturers. The golf club manufacturers really want you to believe that if you purchase their product, you will drive the ball further without taking the time to improve your swing. Similarly, banks and investment companies would like you to believe that just purchasing a new product will solve your financial problems. You know and I know that is just not true.

There are no guarantees with respect to the exact output of any particular product. If you can identify the best strategies—those that are effective under the greatest variety of circumstances—you will give yourself the greatest opportunity for success and lower your risk in the process. Then, and only then, will you have the confidence that comes from knowing that you have made choices superior to all others, based on your own specific requirements. You will sleep better at night when you know that you have done everything you can to minimize your risk.

Part 6:
Protection

Before You Get On The Flying Trapeze, Make Sure They Put Up The Safety Net

My philosophy is simple: protect what you have before you go and get more. Unless you protect what you currently own, your financial foundation will always be at risk. That is no way to get rich and stay rich—and it certainly will not help you sleep nights.

Traditional financial planning rests on the assumption that nothing bad will ever happen. But bad things do happen—car accidents, sickness, injury, market downturns and death. Failing to prepare sensibly for these potential crises (which we hope will never happen) can exact a steep price from you and from those you love.

How Insurance Works

When Vince Lombardi was the coach of the Green Bay Packers, he would begin training camp the same way every season. He would pick up a football and he would say, "Gentlemen, this is a football."

Okay, maybe he left out the word "gentlemen," but he always started with the fundamentals.

You probably know a lot of what I am about to share with you, but as long as we are talking about a topic as important as protection, we should start with the fundamentals too.

Insurance follows the "law of large numbers." It allows an individual person to shift the risk that an event will occur onto an entire group of people. Thus, each person in the group carries a small amount of risk rather than the whole risk falling on a particular member of the group. By doing this, each member can pay a small amount of money to set up a fund that will be paid to the individual or individuals who actually suffer the loss. When you buy insurance, your buying decision should not be based on the cost of the premium; instead, your decision should be based on replacing the lost item or individual economically.

One should not seek to cover the first dollar of loss. To do so would be just too expensive. Instead, you should insure against the larger catastrophe. It makes much more sense to self-insure those losses that will have little impact on your wealth, happiness or success. Therefore, keep the deductible on property and casualty policies, like automobile and home insurance, as high as you can afford. The deductible is the amount you will have to pay out of pocket before the insurance company pays for the rest of any damage claim. As a rule, the higher the deductible, the lower the premium.

Simply by raising the deductibles on your current insurance policies, you may be able to create enough savings to pay for the other kinds of insurance policies I will recommend in this section. This will afford you the opportunity to have greater protection with no additional out-of-pocket cost.

Another important consideration is liability protection. This protects your assets against claims for negligent acts you might commit that could result in damages to someone else's property or injury or death to someone. There is no point in working hard all of your life to build wealth, only to leave yourself exposed to losing it all in a heartbeat.

The Dream Defendant And Auto Insurance

Interested in seeing the dream defendant in a car accident case?

Look in the mirror; it is you.

It is the dream of every personal injury attorney to have a client who gets hit by someone like you—a high income, high net worth individual. If you are driving a BMW or a Mercedes, in the eyes of a plaintiff's attorney, you are a gravy train. So how do you protect yourself, not just from the crazy drivers on the road, but also from their attorneys?

Liability Insurance

Get the most protection that you can get, which is typically, $500,000 of liability protection. This can be expressed either as $500,000 per accident, or $250,000/$500,000, which means that the limit that your insurance company will pay per person for a particular accident is $250,000, and the aggregate limit for any accident is $500,000. Get more if it is available, but do not get any less.

Uninsured/Underinsured Coverage

With this coverage, if an uninsured or underinsured driver hits you, your insurance company pays *you*. It is ironic that many people have higher insurance coverage for strangers than for themselves. It is a travesty because it costs no more than a few dollars a year for you to raise your uninsured/ underinsured coverage to the same level as your liability coverage. This is a very small amount of money to pay for a very large pay-off and it is, after all, for your own protection.

Keep your deductible high

Have a high deductible so you do not trade dollars with the insurance company. Most people have a deductible of $500. I always ask my clients, "How much damage has to happen to your car before you would report the accident to your insurance carrier?" Most people respond, "A couple of thousand dollars" because they know that when they report an accident to the insurance company, even if it is not their fault, their premiums can go up.

If you are willing to absorb "a couple of thousand dollars," then I highly recommend that you have at least a $1,000 deductible. By raising your deductible from $500 to $1,000 you will typically save between $200 and $250 per year on your auto insurance premium. If you do not have an accident for two and one-half years, you will have made your money back. Since you would not report an accident that caused $500 worth of damage, why are you paying for the privilege of doing so?

Keep in mind that your automobile insurance is not there for the little bumps in the road. It is there for the big problems that could take a large chunk out of your net worth. With proper coverage, if you ever get into an accident, you may still be someone's dream defendant, but it will not turn into a nightmare for you.

Keep A Disposable Camera In Your Car

There are three great reasons why you should keep a disposable camera in your car:

First, you might be with your kids or grandkids and they may do something really cute. If you left your camera at home you would lose out on capturing an unforgettable moment. Keeping a disposable camera on hand means that no memory will ever be lost.

Second, if you get a parking ticket and want to fight it, you can show the court exactly where your car was parked. A picture, after all, is worth a thousand words.

Third, if you get into an accident, do not say a word. Do not apologize. Do not say something nice like, "It was all my fault." That can and will be used against you in a court of law! Instead of talking, start shooting ... photographs. Take pictures of the accident from every angle. Once they tow the cars away, it is your word against the other person's word and possibly against the word of the police officer who may or may not see things your way.

Do not rely on your cell phone, even if it has a camera feature in it. Cell phones are not always reliable; sometimes we leave the house without our cell phones; sometimes the battery dies or the pictures are low quality. You do not want to be caught without the ability to take pictures. If the pictures are bad for your case, you can opt not to use them, but you will never have another chance to take them.

I was sitting in my office one morning with a client when his cell phone rang. His daughter was calling from college. She was driving on a main road with no traffic lights or stop signs. As she passed a police station, an off duty police officer came out of the driveway and hit her car broadside. The other police officers came out of the station and began to write up the accident as if it were her fault! Imagine that! Armed with a camera and following the advice to say nothing, my client's daughter took her pictures. Those pictures were the difference between getting her damages paid for and a whole lot of liability.

Home Insurance

Your homeowner's policy combines a number of different coverages. If done properly, it fully replaces the value of your home, its contents and other personal property in the event of damage or destruction. Moreover, it provides liability protection for accidents.

The liability coverage on your home and car should match. If you have a $500,000 liability limit on your car, you should have the same limit with respect to your home. I often see people with $100,000/$300,000 liability coverage on their car and $500,000 on their house. My advice to those people: if you hit someone with your car near your home, drag them into your driveway and run over them again. Of course, I am not serious about this, but it does make the point of why you should have the same liability protection no matter where you are.

Stick With One Company

Generally, when you have the same insurance company insure both your car and your home, you get a discount. It might be only ten percent, but ten percent is nothing to sneer at. That ten percent may make it cost effective to use the same company for both home and auto insurance.

This may not be the case all of the time, so be careful. Some automobile insurance carriers may be less expensive than others even without the discount. Another question you should always ask yourself is: Will this company pay a claim if I have one? You need to be confident in how your insurance company handles claims because that is when you need them the most. What good is cheap automobile insurance if the company will not pay at claim time? All companies are not created equal.

"I Got This At Tiffany's ..."

Keep an inventory of all the valuables (furniture, clothing and anything else worth real money) in your home. Keep your receipts for high-ticket items and take videos of all of your possessions. If you have kids, you have a video camera. If you do not have a video camera, borrow one from your neighbor. Walk around your house and record everything that is worth anything. Be sure to keep the receipts and the videotapes somewhere *outside* of your home. Keep it in the home of a relative; put it in your safe deposit box; keep it at work. You do not want the record of what you own burning down with your house and your possessions!

Finally, make sure your home is insured for its full replacement cost. That way if it burns down, the insurance company will build or buy you a new home that is as nice as, or maybe even nicer than, the one you lost.

Smile ... You Have A Liability Umbrella

For $200 to $250 per year, you can usually buy the biggest bargain in the insurance world—$1,000,000 worth of "liability umbrella" protection. A liability umbrella sits over your home and car insurance and will kick in after you have used up the underlying coverage on either of these primary policies.

A liability umbrella may also provide you with broader coverage than your homeowner's and automobile policies offer. For example, the umbrella often includes coverage for bodily injury, property damage and personal injury. Personal injury is not often included in automobile or homeowner coverages and may include protection for things like false arrest or false imprisonment, malicious prosecution, defamation, invasion of privacy, wrongful entry and more.

I have $5,000,000 of umbrella coverage. The first million costs me $234 dollars per year. The last million costs only about twenty-five dollars per year. The total cost for the $5,000,000 of umbrella coverage is approximately $750. If I cause a car accident, or if somebody slips and falls in my house, my assets are protected up to the amount of my $5,000,000 liability umbrella. Not until the umbrella coverage is exhausted can the attorney for the injured person start looking at my other assets. Five million dollars of my net worth is protected because I spend $750 dollars per year on that liability umbrella.

Think about it this way: if you take the $250 that you saved by raising the deductible on your auto insurance from $500 to $1,000, you can use that $250 to buy $1,000,000 of umbrella coverage. What is more efficient: spending $250 to protect $500 on your car deductible or spending the same $250 to protect $1,000,000 of your assets? Get yourself a liability umbrella and do not leave home without it.

Disability Insurance

Unfortunately, people in our society get sick and injured. Most people think that sickness or injury does not happen to young people. Moreover, people assume that when it does, it is the result of a job-related incident. These beliefs are not true. In fact, your odds of getting sick or injured before age sixty-five and having the condition last for ninety days or more, are as follows:

Age	Odds of sickness or injury	Average duration
30	1 in 3	32 months
40	3 in 10	42 months
50	5 in 22	50 months
60	1 in 10	54 months[1]

---

1. "Commissioner's Disability Table, 1985", and "Commissioner's Standard Mortality Table, 1980".

Fewer than fourteen percent of all long-term disabilities are caused by injuries. And even when the disabilities are caused by injury, most of those injuries do not occur in the workplace. In fact, the vast majority of disabled people become disabled due to illness.[2]

If you do not have enough assets to support you for the rest of your life, then you need disability insurance. Forty-nine percent of all home foreclosures in the United States result from individuals becoming sick or injured on the job, in a car accident or by some other means.[3] Like other insurance, the amount of disability protection you get should cover the full value of your lost income—the full economic replacement cost. Why would you want you or your family to have a lower standard of living simply because you have become sick or injured?

Ideally, you should have a personally owned disability policy. Group disability policies, like the ones offered by associations or employers, have many disadvantages. As I will discuss below, the definition of disability is often not favorable and it may change after a certain time. Additionally, these plans do not typically protect against inflation or provide lifetime coverage. They also integrate with other benefits, which may further reduce the amount you get paid if you become sick or injured.

---

2.   "U.S. Department of Education, National Institute on Disability and Rehabilitation Research", 1999.
3.   "Compton Insurance Marketing", 2002.

In employer plans, the amount of coverage that is offered is often tied to your base salary and will therefore not include your bonus, which could be a substantial part of your compensation. Moreover, since your employer is providing the plan, any money you receive under the plan may be taxable as if it had been earned income. Such plans are also not typically portable—meaning that if you leave your job, the plan does not come with you. This is a problem because there may be a waiting period in your next job or no coverage at all. Your best bet is to purchase a private policy so that you are guaranteed coverage no matter what your employer provides.

Let's dig a little deeper into what disability insurance is all about.

Here is a simple exercise: hold your hands up in front of you. In your left hand imagine that you are holding all of the assets you have acquired to this date—all the money you have made in your entire lifetime so far.

In your right hand, imagine that you are holding all of the assets that you will acquire from now until the day you quit working.

Which hand is heavier? If you are like most people, you have a strange sense that the right hand—the hand that contains all of the money you are *going to make* is the heavier hand. Doesn't it make sense to protect that right hand? Your earning potential is the most valuable asset you own—far more valuable than your car, your home or perhaps even your current investment portfolio.

I like to share with my clients a simple metaphor. Let's assume that there is a factory which is responsible for the entire profit of a company. Let's further assume that this factory has one special machine that produces everything in the factory. Wouldn't it be in that company's best interest to have a backup machine in case the first machine breaks down, an insurance policy on that machine or at a minimum, a service contract to make sure that machine continues to function?

Isn't your income-producing ability just like that machine?

Disability insurance is something that people do not want to think about. No one wants to think about being sick or injured, but it is imperative to consider this possibility. Disability insurance is a cost, but it is a cost worth paying.

If you totaled your car tomorrow, your car insurance would pay for a new car minus your deductible. If your house burned down tomorrow, the insurance company would replace it as well. Those are two pretty big assets. Yet, your ability to earn money is your biggest asset of all. If that went away tomorrow, where would you be? If you really want to protect what you own, protect your ability to keep making money. You accomplish that with disability insurance.

Your ability to make money is something that cannot be replaced without disability insurance. For example, a forty year-old dentist gets blindsided by a drunk driver. He survives the accident, but he cannot work anymore. He had just gotten to the point where he had paid off his student loans and his practice had just begun to experience tremendous growth. Nevertheless, his earning years are over. Consider all his education, all his training and all the effort he used to build his practice. And consider the reality that now he cannot earn another dollar practicing dentistry. If you were that dentist, wouldn't you wish you had purchased disability insurance?

Some people argue against purchasing disability insurance because they rely on the fact that, most likely, they will never see a return on the money spent to buy the policy. I truly *hope* you never see a return on your disability insurance premiums, but if you ever need it, you will be happy that you have it. You have car insurance because the state in which you live requires it. You have home insurance because you could not have obtained a mortgage without it. Those are checks you write that do not buy anything tangible, like a Rolex or a new suit or dress. However, you write them to protect against the loss of something very important to you. So the question becomes obvious: why aren't you protecting your greatest asset—your ability to earn money—in the same fashion?

You should purchase as much disability insurance benefit as the insurance company will issue to you. If you pay the premium with after-tax dollars, the benefit—that monthly income you will receive—is non-taxable. If you pay with pre-tax dollars, the benefit is taxable. So, if at all possible, you want to buy disability insurance with after-tax dollars. You should be aware that there are limits to the coverage that you can purchase. For some occupations the limit may be $10,000 to $15,000 per month (assuming you qualify medically and financially).

You might say, "Mitch, I am used to making $40,000 a month. What good is $10,000 or $15,000?" My answer to you is that it is a whole lot better than nothing, which is what you would be making if you were totally disabled. It may not get you all the way to "whole," but it will get you as close as the law will allow.

Here are some of the issues to consider when buying a disability policy:

1. **Deductible**—In a disability insurance policy, the deductible is expressed as the number of days the insured individual is sick or injured before the policy starts paying benefits. You can get a thirty-day deductible, but it is very expensive. I typically advise my clients to self-insure the first ninety days and let the disability insurance take over after the ninety-day period. You should have a "slush fund" in place to pay for those first ninety days after a disabling accident. The ninety-day deductible is much more cost effective. Remember, your policy should have a high deductible with full economic replacement.

2. **How much benefit?** Get as much as you can!

3. **"Future increase option"**—For a small amount of money you can purchase this option to increase your "bottom line benefit"—the amount of money you will

receive each month if you are sick or injured—without having to go through the process of testing your health for insurability. In other words, if you buy a policy now, you have to demonstrate to the insurance company that you are insurable—i.e. that you are healthy, that you do not take any insane risks with your life (like bungee jumping or skydiving) and that you qualify financially. With the future increase option, you can typically increase the size of your benefit without going through the insurability process again. The only thing you will have to prove is that you qualify financially.

4. **"Own occupation" disability definition**—This is a little bit of insurance mumbo jumbo that will mean a lot to you if you ever become sick or injured. There are three definitions of disability in disability policies. One definition of disability is "own occupation." This is the kind of policy you want. With the "own occupation" definition, the insurance company will look at you and ask, "Can you perform the activity for which you are employed?" For example, if you are a neurosurgeon and your hands start to shake and you lose the ability to use your hands, the disability payments flow to you. The second definition is "any occupation." With an "any occupation" definition, if you are working in any capacity and earning money, the insurance company will not pay you benefits. For example, if you are a surgeon and you cannot operate but you are gainfully employed teaching, you will not be

paid insurance benefits even though you make far less money teaching. Third, there is the definition used by the Social Security Administration. Under this definition, you only collect benefits if you cannot do *anything at all*. If a neurosurgeon had the social security definition of disability, the insurance company would say, "Sure, he cannot be a neurosurgeon anymore, but he could still push a broom. Benefits denied!" Sound ludicrous? Yes. For this reason, you must choose a disability policy that employs the "own occupation" definition of disability.

5. **Inflation protection**—Buy a cost of living rider. This rider raises the benefit by some factor every year while you are collecting benefits. It increases with the cost of living. If the sickness or injury lasts a long time, you will need to keep pace with inflation. What if you are sick or injured for twenty years or more?

Nobody wants to think about disability insurance. However, no one who has it and needs it regrets that they took the time to think it through, nor do they ever regret the money they spent to buy it.

Cannot Get Much Disability Insurance? What's Up Doc?

Once upon a time, there were dozens of quality insurance companies offering disability insurance. Now there are just a few good ones left. Why is this? Unfortunately, it is a result of the medical profession's attempt to deal with the exorbitant costs of their malpractice insurance premiums and the insurance companies' success at continually limiting their profits. Doctors came to realize that they could make as much or more money collecting benefits under their disability income policies as they could actually practicing medicine. As such, great numbers of doctors "gamed the system" and claimed disability—and while wrestling with their consciences, they enjoyed the benefit of a nice insurance income every month.

Today, only a handful of companies like Berkshire Life Insurance Company, Massachusetts Mutual, MetLife and Northwestern Mutual still offer good disability insurance policies. Every year, these companies keep cutting back on the benefits they offer in order to stay profitable; so buy now!

Insuring Your Health

Medical or Health Insurance

Health care costs are skyrocketing, and one serious illness can put a major dent in your finances, if not bankrupt you altogether. People are living longer, thus increasing the probability that they will have a serious illness. Medical science helps people live with serious illnesses that previously would have killed them. In light of all these facts, it is important to have good medical coverage and to understand the coverage that you have. Medical insurance protects your assets from loss due to the cost of treatment for sickness or injury. It is available on an individual or group basis, and it provides coverage for such things as doctor's fees, hospital stays, in-hospital expenses, mental health care, treatment for substance abuse and supplemental services like prescription drugs and blood work.

Whether your plan is a "reimbursement plan" (also known as an "indemnity plan") or a managed care plan, if you have private coverage, you should consider raising your deductible the same way you do for your automobile and homeowner's insurance. You should also know whether there is a lifetime cap on your policy benefits and if so, what that cap is. This is important because if one of the people insured under your plan has an illness that would cause you to exceed the cap under your current policy, you should know this long before your benefits run out. This way you can do some immediate planning to help preserve your assets, which may include, among other things, obtaining government assistance. Make sure that your health care policy has a significant lifetime cap—at least $1,000,000.

Long-Term Care Insurance

Long-term care is the care provided when someone can no longer independently carry out the essential "activities of daily living" on his or her own. For long-term care purposes, the activities of daily living are eating, bathing, dressing, toileting, transferring (moving from a bed to a chair and back) and continence. By the year 2020, twelve million Americans will require long-term care.[4]

---

4.   "A Guide to Long-Term Care Insurance", c 2004 America's Health Insurance Plans.

Traditionally, women in the United States have provided this care to their family members. However, today more women work outside of the home and families tend to be more geographically scattered. Additionally, giving full-time care to a loved one can be both physically and emotionally draining for the caregiver. Moreover, no one who requires long-term care wants to be "a burden" on his or her family. As a result, more people are turning to outside caregivers. Long-term care is expensive. Medicare is not designed to pay for long-term care expenses and therefore will cover little, if any, of the expenses incurred.[5] Medicaid will pay for "approved" long-term care expenses; however, it is only available to people who fall under the Medicaid definition of "indigent."[6]

If you have considerable wealth and are able to self-insure for these potential expenses, you may not need long-term care insurance. However, your wealth does not change the fact that the cost of an unexpected medical crisis is extremely high. In fact, it can wipe out a considerable amount of wealth in a relatively short span of time. Therefore, long-term care insurance is something well worth considering.

---

5.   "A Guide to Long-Term Care Insurance", c 2004 America's Health Insurance Plans.

6.   "A Guide to Long-Term Care Insurance", c 2004 America's Health Insurance Plans.

Wills—You Have To Have One!

While discussing protection, we need to spend a moment talking about wills. A will is a written and executed document that directs your executor or executrix to gather and then distribute the assets that are in your estate upon your death according to your wishes. The executor or executrix is the person you choose to carry out this task. Among other things, a will can help reduce estate taxes and create trusts to provide income to individuals or charities.

There are many decisions you need to make when creating a will. Perhaps the most important decision you will make if you have minor children is deciding who will be their guardian in the event that something happens to you and your spouse. Who will raise your children? This is a decision you should make now; it is not a decision that you want left to a court if you die without a guardianship provision in your will. Not being able to agree on a guardian is no reason to put off making a will. While no one will raise your children as well as you will, you need to, at the very least, express your feelings as to who would do the best job. Plus, you can always change your will if the original guardian you choose is no longer a viable option. Other than asking your guardian if they will accept the responsibility, it is nobody's business who you choose. You do not have to worry about offending anyone by not choosing them as guardian because if your will becomes public record, you are gone and do not have to worry about the wrath of a spurned relative or friend.

The next issue to consider is who should be the trustee of your children's money? It may be wise to have a trustee who is not the same person as the guardian, thus setting up a system of "checks and balances." If you and your spouse were to perish, your children may be too young to handle the responsibility of large sums of money designed to last them a long time.

Similarly, it is up to you to decide when your children should get their money. In some states, eighteen year-olds can receive the entirety of their parents' estate. In other states, the legal age is twenty-one. Think back to the time when you were eighteen, or even twenty-one years old. How responsible were you? If you had been given a multimillion-dollar bequest, would it have gone into sound investments or might it have been spent on the beaches in Cancun? Often the best solution is to give children money over a period of time. For example, you can distribute a third of the trust at age twenty-five, half of what is left at age thirty and the rest at age thirty-five.

Despite the distribution ages, the trustees should be permitted to invade the trust for the health, education and welfare of your children. Then, if your child is mature and wants the money, or is going to graduate school and needs the money, the trustee can invade the principal for your child's benefit. Conversely, if your child is immature, the trustee can point to the language of the trust and say, "Mom and Dad explained how and when you should get the money, and you are not yet entitled to it." The trustee can use the trust language as a shield for your assets and can therefore protect your children from themselves, from creditors and from unhappy spouses, if need be.

A proper will, combined with the proper ownership of assets, can make it possible for you to shelter substantially more assets from estate taxation. I do not want to delve too deeply into the topic mostly because it is very complex and because the attorney who writes and helps you execute your will and/or your own financial planner should cover this. Nevertheless, it is important to maximize your "applicable exclusion." The estate tax laws of the United States allow each of us to shelter a sum of assets from federal estate taxes. This is now commonly referred to as the "applicable exclusion." It used to be called the "unified credit."

Unfortunately, without proper planning, the first spouse to die will waste their applicable exclusion. Each spouse is entitled to his or her own applicable exclusion. Typically, the first spouse to die leaves all of their assets to the surviving spouse. Under current law, these assets pass from spouse to spouse estate tax-free. When the surviving spouse dies, he or she gets to protect an amount equal to the applicable exclusion from federal estate taxes. Thus, the couple has only taken advantage of the exclusion one time; the first spouse's applicable exclusion is lost forever.

To prevent this waste, both spouses' wills should set up a trust that, upon death, can house assets equal to the applicable exclusion. This trust can have several names: credit shelter trust, uniform bypass credit trust or disclaimer trust. Typically, the trust is written in such a way as to allow the surviving spouse to draw both principal and interest from the trust in order to keep him or her living "in the style to which he or she has become accustomed" if need be. Drawing money from this trust should be discretionary, not mandatory. After all, it makes no sense to bring money which has escaped estate taxes back into an estate, where it will be taxed, if it is not needed.

When the second spouse dies, the assets remaining in the trust can pass to the children with no estate tax consequences, together with the second spouse's applicable exclusion. This technique allows a couple to shelter twice as many assets from federal estate taxation (see Figure 6.1).

While preparing your will, you should also create living wills, health care proxies and powers of attorney. The living will and health care proxy are documents appointing a representative to make health-care decisions regarding extraordinary life-support measures in the event of an accident or illness that leaves you without the capacity to make those decisions yourself. The last thing you want is to have your relatives fighting at the hospital regarding your care in the event that you are comatose or otherwise unable to speak or act for yourself. Though unpleasant, this is another one of those issues that you would rather have handled a decade early than a minute too late.

A power of attorney is a written document that gives a person the power to act on your behalf. It can be general and apply to all of your affairs or specific and apply only to certain enumerated issues. The power of attorney can also be durable (meaning that it is in force all of the time) or it can be "springing" and only takes effect when a specific set of circumstances arise, like mental incapacity.

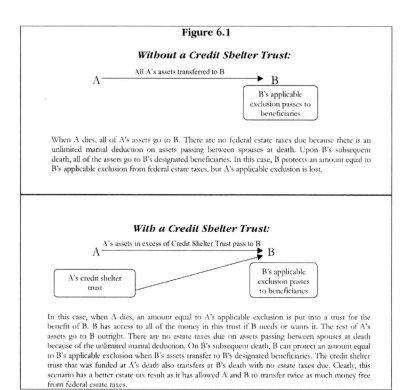

Figure 6.1

Without a Credit Shelter Trust:

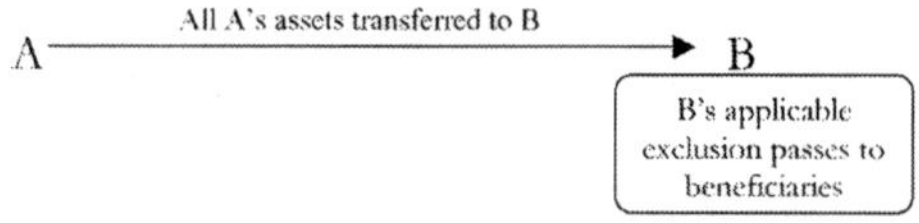
All A's assets transferred to B
A
B
B's applicable exclusion passes to beneficiaries

When A dies, all of A's assets go to B. There are no federal estate taxes due because there is an unlimited marital deduction on assets passing between spouses at death. Upon B's subsequent death, all of the assets go to B's designated beneficiaries. In this case, B protects an amount equal to B's applicable exclusion from federal estate taxes, but A's applicable exclusion is lost.

With a Credit Shelter Trust:

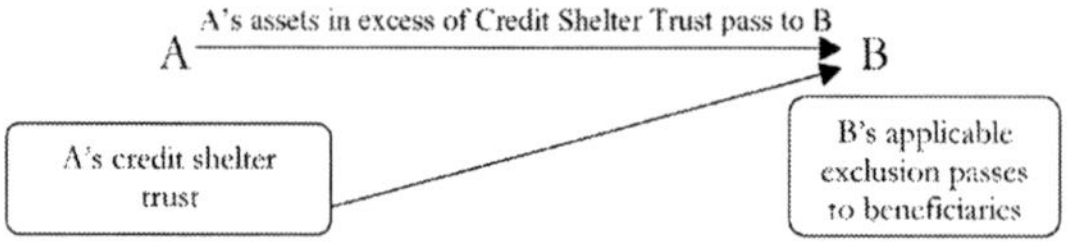
A's assets in excess of Credit Shelter Trust pass to B
A
B
A's credit shelter trust
B's applicable exclusion passes to beneficiaries

In this case, when A dies, an amount equal to A's applicable exclusion is put into a trust for the benefit of B. B has access to all of the money in this trust if B needs or wants it. The rest of A's assets go to B outright. There are no estate taxes due on assets passing between spouses at death because of the unlimited marital deduction. On B's subsequent death, B can protect an amount equal to B's applicable exclusion when B's assets transfer to B's designated beneficiaries. The credit shelter trust that was funded at A's death also transfers at B's death with no estate taxes due. Clearly, this scenario has a better estate tax result as it has allowed A and B to transfer twice as much money free from federal estate taxes.

Life Insurance

What would you call someone who left their family in the middle of the night, with no money and a ton of debt? You might call them selfish, thoughtless or callous. You might also call them the victim of a heart attack, a stroke, a car accident or some other unforeseen tragedy. Your goal is to insure your income stream so that if this tragedy happens to you, your family will be able to keep their home and the lifestyle to which they have become accustomed. One simple strategy is to have enough life insurance to make that possible. However, "needs analysis"—the approach of the traditional financial planner—is seldom accurate. With respect to life insurance, traditional "needs analysis" puts the emphasis on the needs of the beneficiary rather than the value of the insured. You should look to insure your future income stream, not to make sure that your family's current financial obligations are satisfied. Keep in mind that had you lived, your income would have increased over time so that your family could have enjoyed an even nicer lifestyle, paid for college for the children, bought a second home and so on. Therefore, your life insurance should replace you economically. Specifically, this means replacing your future income stream.

An insurance company will not issue an infinite amount of insurance on your life. They do not want it to be too advantageous for you to disappear. Instead, they will generally cap your life insurance death benefit at approximately twenty times your gross income if you are between the ages of twenty-five and forty. If you are between forty and fifty-five years old, the cap is about fifteen times your gross income. If you are fifty-five years of age or older and still working, insurance companies will likely cap your benefit at ten times your gross income. If you are retired, the maximum amount of life insurance an insurance company will typically issue on your life is equal to the value of your net worth.

What Are You Really Worth?

When it comes to most areas of insurance, people naturally tend to buy the maximum amount of protection they need to replace whatever is lost. If your house burned down tomorrow, would you want your insurance policy to cover the rebuilding of the entire house or just a couple of rooms? If your car were stolen, would you want the insurance company to pay you for the entire value of the car or for just one wheel?

Naturally, people want their homes and cars insured in a way that provides maximum protection. So why don't people do the same thing with their lives?

This leads to the integral issue of how to value a human life. From a spiritual point of view, the value of a human life is infinite. But as a practical matter, insurance companies and the courts have to deal with the value of a life in purely economic terms. Let's say that an individual is hit and killed by a truck belonging to a Fortune 500 company. In a situation where a defendant has "deep pockets," would the surviving spouse of that individual sue for a small amount of money or for everything they could get?

Assuming that the driver killed the person due to negligent operation of the truck, the spouse would sue the Fortune 500 company for every possible dollar. How will the court determine how much money the spouse will receive? Each side will bring in experts to testify about the economic value of the life of the deceased. In the end, courts will generally settle on an award equal to ten to twenty times the annual income of the deceased depending on his or her age.

Is ten to twenty times your annual income enough to meet the needs of your family far into the future? Will your surviving spouse be able to afford the home, the way of life and the education of your children in a manner that would have been possible had you lived? I always advise my clients to get all the protection they can. People buy home insurance to replace their whole house and automobile insurance to replace their entire car. Similarly, they should get the maximum amount of life insurance that insurance companies will issue. Only then can they hope to adequately meet the financial responsibilities facing their family long after they are gone.

How Much Insurance Is Enough?

High-income individuals between the ages of thirty-five and fifty-five need to know how much life insurance they can get. Whenever I sit down with a person and that person tells me how much life insurance they have, I always ask the same question: "Is that too much, too little or the right amount?"

They usually answer, "I don't know."

So I say, "Let's talk about it. What would happen if you died?"

The primary purpose of life insurance is to replace a person economically. So in economic terms, we are insuring that person as an income stream. Generally, the older a person is, the less life insurance there is available to that person. Insurance companies assume that as you age, you have less earning years left. In the eyes of an insurance company, as you age, your human life value actually decreases. Let's take a look at the numbers.

Let's consider an individual who is earning $500,000 a year. At that income level, a thirty-five year-old would be able to purchase ten million dollars of life insurance. A forty-five year-old would be able to purchase seven and one-half million dollars of life insurance and a fifty-five year-old would be able to purchase five million dollars of life insurance.

For individuals earning $1,000,000 a year, the numbers double: a thirty-five year-old could buy twenty million dollars of life insurance, a forty-five year-old, fifteen million dollars of life insurance, and a fifty-five year-old can purchase ten million dollars of life insurance.

How much do you earn and how much life insurance would it take to replace your income now and in the future?

Types Of Life Insurance

Term Life Insurance

Term life insurance provides a death benefit for a specified period of time. Term life insurance pays only if you die during the "term" of the policy. The premium may be level for a period of time, or it can increase yearly. It builds no cash value. The death benefit on term life insurance can stay level or even decline.

The advantage of term life insurance is that the initial cost of the life insurance is lower because you are paying only for the protection. There is no cash value or investment component. As mentioned earlier, this is a short-term solution to a specific need. Less than two percent of term life insurance policies ever pay a death benefit because either the term expires or the increasing premiums on the policy make it unaffordable to keep beyond the initial term period.[7] Therefore, whenever you buy a term life insurance policy, always choose policies that are convertible into whole life insurance without having to prove insurability. This will guarantee your right to convert your term policy into whole life insurance even if you are not as healthy as you were when you purchased the initial policy. You should make sure that the company from which you purchase term life insurance is

---

7.   Penn State University, "1993 Study on the Fate of Term Insurance Policy".

strong enough financially to warrant you purchasing a permanent product from it in the future.

Universal Life Insurance

Universal life insurance is term life insurance combined with an investment component. It typically has a lower premium per dollar of death benefit than whole life insurance and offers flexibility of premium payments. Universal life pays an interest rate on the cash value in the investment portion of the policy. The interest rate that the insurance company pays changes annually or semi-annually, depending on the policy. The rate is based on the return of the general account of the insurance company.

Universal life has three sets of guarantees built into the policy. The first is the guaranteed interest rate. This is the minimum rate that can be credited to the policy and varies from company to company. Second is the guaranteed mortality rate, which is based on a table of mortality required by the various state insurance departments. The third guarantee is the guaranteed expense charges, which are the amounts that the insurance company charges for administering the policy. Despite these guarantees, the reliance on the return of the general account of the insurance company means that the premium, cash value and death benefit cannot be guaranteed. Therefore, the "investment" risk in these policies is borne by the insured rather than the insurance company.

Nevertheless, the account value increases with premium payments and interest that is credited to the policy, and it decreases with mortality costs and policy expense charges. The insurance company, subject to the maximums guaranteed in the insurance contract, can change the mortality and expense charges as conditions change.

Since there is no guaranteed premium, cash value or death benefit, the major concern of universal life insurance policyholders should be that the policy will lapse if the cash value falls to zero. This can happen if the policy was inadequately funded, meaning that there was not enough money paid into the policy or that the interest credited was lower than originally projected. As such, universal life may not be an appropriate insurance policy to use for tax strategies with respect to your qualified plan, other retirement planning, estate planning or charitable giving because the death benefit may not be there when you are counting on it the most.

Variable Life

Like universal life insurance, variable life insurance is made up of term life insurance and an investment vehicle. The difference is that with variable life, the investment component offers the owner of the policy a choice of several different mutual funds. The theory here is that because the investment is in mutual funds, driven by the stock and bond markets, the cash value in variable life policies may grow more than the cash value in universal life insurance or whole life insurance policies. Conversely though, this feature also puts the cash value of the policy at more risk. If the markets are unkind, they can put the life insurance at risk of lapse.

With variable life insurance policies, there are only two guarantees: the guaranteed mortality rate, based on a table of mortality required by the various state insurance departments and the guaranteed expense charges, the amounts that the insurance company charges for administering the policy.

In the case of variable life insurance, as in the case of universal life insurance, the investment risk is shifted to the insured and away from the insurance company. If the stock market declines or does not do as well as projected, the company may require you to pay premiums in excess of the amount quoted when the policy was purchased. Your policy's death benefit may be reduced or the policy may even lapse!

Since the growth of its cash value is not certain or guaranteed in any way, variable life insurance is even less appropriate than universal life insurance with respect to your financial and estate planning.

Whole Life Insurance

Whole life insurance is a policy that provides lifetime protection with significant guarantees and tax benefits. In the case of whole life insurance, the company that issues the policy guarantees that, at worst, the premium will stay level (the premium may be reduced or eliminated at some point depending on performance), the death benefit will be there when the insured dies so long as the premiums are paid and there will be a cash value.

Whole life insurance may also perform better than its guarantees promise because it has the ability to produce dividends. Dividends are paid to the policyholders if "declared" by the board of directors of the insurance company. Dividends can be declared for several reasons, one of which is that the insurance company's investment rate of return, mortality experience or expenses of policy administration was better than the minimum guarantee promised in the policy contract. Most good companies never fail to declare a dividend. Once a dividend is declared and that money is added to your cash value, it cannot be taken away.

Survivorship Life Insurance, "Second to Die"

Survivorship life insurance is often used as an estate-planning tool. It is designed to pay the death benefit when the second of two spouses dies. As such, it is typically thought of as a good way to pay the estate tax that would be due at the death of the second spouse. The premium for survivorship life insurance is typically less than the premium for single life life insurance because an additional event (death of the second spouse) must occur before the insurance company has to pay a claim. Therefore, second to die life insurance appeals to many older couples with large illiquid estates who are interested in insuring against the estate tax that may be due upon the death of the second spouse. With second to die life insurance, the heirs will not be forced to liquidate the estate in order to pay the estate tax if the insurance proceeds are sufficient to pay the tax.

Second to die life insurance is not typically appropriate for younger couples because there is a substantial likelihood that at least one spouse will live a long time and there will be a great disparity in lifespans. If that occurs, there is a large lost opportunity cost due to the years of premium payments one spouse will make without any death benefit until the second spouse dies. There is also a chance that, with younger couples, the premium cost and lost opportunity cost on the premiums paid may be greater than the death benefit provided.

As you can tell, I am biased towards whole life insurance. Whole life insurance has more guarantees and is more predictable. It acts as a permission slip for its owner to use other assets in his or her estate much more efficiently. Talk with your advisor about which of these life insurance options is most appropriate for you.

Insuring Your Insurability

This is one of the most important concepts in financial planning. After all, everyone knows you cannot insure a burning building. For a healthy forty-five year-old male, $5,000,000 of twenty-year level term life insurance costs approximately $8,000 a year. For $5,000,000 of whole life insurance, the annual premium is approximately $100,000.

Not all of my clients can afford this huge step up in premiums, and for those who can, some simply do not want to do so. I advise them to buy as much whole life insurance as they can comfortably afford and then supplement that whole life insurance with enough term life insurance (remember it should be convertible) to replace them economically (to the extent possible) in the event of their death.

This accomplishes two things. First, you have protected your family. They will have all of the death benefit they need should the worst happen. Second, you have "insured your insurability." Again, when you buy term life insurance, you should also buy the right to convert the term life insurance policy into a whole life insurance policy, regardless of any changes that may occur in your health.

For most people, their health worsens as they age. Cholesterol levels go up, blood pressure goes up and weight goes up. Essentially, everything you do not want to go up, goes up! Getting insured later in life is harder—and also more expensive—simply because as you age, your chances of dying improve. Therefore, insurance companies look at older, less healthy people as higher risks. The health changes that may occur in the lives of some individuals may actually prevent them from being insurable.

So, when you purchase as much whole life insurance as you can afford and buy term life insurance to make up the difference, you have not only insured your family's well-being, but you have also insured your own insurability.

Part 7:
Debt

The Good, The Bad And The Ugly

Do you remember the Wizard of Oz? There were good witches and bad witches. Debt is a lot like witches—there is good debt and there is bad debt. In this section, I will discuss why debt is not automatically a bad thing. The first thing to know about good debt is that when you borrow money to do something, you are using "OPM"—other people's money—for that investment. With OPM, your investment dollar is not gone forever. When you invest your own money, it very well may be.

Even though corporate America has done this forever, individuals have not applied the same techniques to their personal finances. For instance, it is likely that GE can afford to finance many of its own projects. Nevertheless, GE floats bonds to raise money rather than use its own funds to finance its endeavors. GE knows that it can borrow money at one rate and use the money to obtain a higher rate of return while pocketing the profit. If it works for corporate America, it should work for individuals as well. People fail to apply these principals to their personal life. A perfect example of this is how people treat their mortgages. Most people approach their mortgage from an emotional rather than a financial point of view. Our parents and grandparents have taught us that it is a good thing to pay off our homes as quickly as possible. What motivates us to act in this manner? We believe, or have been taught, that if our house is paid off, we will never lose it. However, the risks inherent in home ownership do not go away even if you make your regular mortgage payments to the bank. The idea of paying off your house so that you cannot lose it is actually one of the last vestiges of Depression-era thinking. Let's take a deeper look at why it is so common for the children and grandchildren of those who survived the Depression to have this attitude.

Part of what made the "Roaring Twenties" roar was the practice of "margin" buying. You could control $10 dollars worth of stock for every dollar that you actually had invested in the market. When the market began to drop, long before "Black Friday" in October of 1929, brokers issued margin calls to their clients. In other words, the value of stocks declined slightly at first, and investors had to put actual dollars into the stock market to solidify their hold on their investments. Most people did not want to sell declining stock, figuring that their stock investments would rebound. Instead, they took their savings to pay their margin calls.

With the great amounts of money people were withdrawing from banks, the banks began to face a liquidity crisis of their own. Banks then looked to their portfolios to see which assets were the most liquid and could therefore be quickly turned into cash. The answer was home mortgages. Banks began "calling" home loans, demanding that people pay off the balance on their mortgages immediately. Most people, of course, could not do so any more than most people today could pay off their entire mortgage. Since they could not pay off their entire mortgage, they lost their homes to the bank.

Consequently, as stock and home prices sank, the unemployment rate soared. In an illiquid investment environment, companies could not afford to expand their business. In many cases, the companies could not afford to do business at all. As a result, many people lost their jobs or could not find jobs. Banks were failing, homeowners were losing their homes (further driving down the value of homes) and businesses could neither borrow money from banks to do business (because the banks had no money to lend) nor find customers to buy their goods and services (because so many people had lost everything, including their jobs, savings and homes).

In short, if you had a mortgage, the bank could take away your house—and wipe you out—at any time. Those who survived the Depression advised their children and grandchildren to pay off their mortgages so this could never happen to them. The specter of so many Americans losing their homes to this kind of situation caused Congress to pass laws that now make it illegal for banks to "call" mortgage loans just because the banks need money. Thus, what happened in 1929 and the early 1930s could never happen again. That paradigm simply does not exist today. No matter how far down the stock market might drop, and no matter what liquidity crisis your bank might face, your bank no longer has the right to call your home mortgage. Banks cannot turn to homeowners as a method of staving off their own cash crunches. So, as much as you understand the reason why your parents and grandparents want you to pay off your mortgage as quickly as possible, it no longer makes economic sense. What happened back then simply cannot happen now.

Today we can, and in fact should, look at mortgage debt differently. If you have more money than you owe on your loan, then you are not really in debt! You have made a financial choice. You may have some debt on your balance sheet, but you are not a "net debtor." This is a different definition of debt from the one that our parents and grandparents had traditionally used.

Investing In Home Equity

Many people think that home ownership provides a great rate of return on their equity. In fact, the rate of return on home equity is less than zero. First, you get zero interest on your down payment; so, already you are losing to inflation. Second, houses are expensive to maintain and property taxes are not cheap either. The same money that you use to fix up your house could have been invested. Although you may obtain emotional value from a more attractive or livable home, from a strictly economic point of view, that fixed-up porch has a current rate of return that is less than zero because all the money that you sunk into your house is gone until you sell it, and you may not be able to retrieve it even then.

Let's look at an example. Take two identical houses on the same block that sold for $500,000 each. Ethel put down $100,000 when she bought her house. Fred, her next-door neighbor, paid all $500,000 in cash. A year later, they each sell their house for $1,000,000.

Who had a better rate of return? Fred is smiling because he made out very well. His investment doubled, earning him a 100% return on his $500,000. But why is Ethel grinning from ear to ear? Ethel is smiling because she put down $100,000 and made 500% on her money—her $100,000 got her a $500,000 return. Nice going, Ethel!

Not only did Ethel make more money, she kept the use and control of the $400,000 that Fred sunk into his house. As a result, she was able to make other investments that also appreciated nicely that year. Who would you rather be, Fred or Ethel?

Or would you rather be Charlie across the street? Charlie paid off his house five years ago. Sure, he thinks he has security and peace of mind; but what about all of the money that he paid into his house? From an investment perspective, he could have done just as well by taking it, putting it in a coffee can and burying it in his front yard. Charlie has actually lost money due to inflation. Hopefully, he can find that coffee can without digging up his entire front lawn. I would rather be Ethel and so should you.

Remember The Good Investment Test

As much as you may love it, the house in which you live fails the three-pronged test of a good investment: it is not liquid, it is not safe and you have no control over the money you have invested in it. As Robert Kiyosaki accurately points out in his book, "Rich Dad, Poor Dad," a house is a liability until the day you sell it. An asset is something that puts money into your pocket; a liability is something that takes money away from you. Accordingly, a house is a liability because, as discussed, it costs you money to keep it—money in the form of taxes, utilities, mortgage payments and repairs.

A good investment is liquid and liquidity breeds safety. Safety does not come from putting as much cash into your mortgage as you can. Safety comes from creating a "side fund" so that you have highly liquid investments you can turn into cash if times get tough. Let's go back to the example of Fred and Ethel from a few moments ago. Fred put his

$500,000 into his house. Assume that instead of the housing market going up, it actually dropped a bit. Fred got a new job and had to relocate to another part of the country. Fred had no other cash on hand to use once relocation became a necessity. Fred was forced to sell his old house at a loss and use the proceeds from the sale to purchase the new house in his new location.

Now, let's turn to Ethel. Same factors—the housing market turned down and she has to move because of her job. Remember, Ethel has that nice big side fund of $400,000. She is not dependent on selling her current house in order to buy her new house. She has more options than Fred. She can hang onto her house or rent it out and wait for the market to come back. Again, wouldn't you rather be Ethel than Fred?

Although it is unimaginable that there could be anything negative about home ownership when you consider the appreciation in home values since 1999, there are other factors that make a house a risky investment. What if unruly neighbors suddenly move into the house next door to you? What if the city decides to build a prison or a halfway house around the corner? We live in an era of acronyms. NIMBY stands for "Not In My Back Yard" and BANANA stands for "Build Absolutely Nothing Anywhere Near Anything." Yet, things do get built that lower housing values, and there is not much you can do about a neighbor's barking dog when you are trying to sell your home.

Disability and job loss are two other important consider-
ations when deciding how much money to put into a house
and how much money to put into a side fund. An industry
source indicates that forty-nine percent of foreclosures in the
United States are due to people becoming sick or injured—a
sudden car accident, a skiing accident or the like.[1] People
who put down too much money on their homes, or seek to
pay off their mortgages too quickly, are looking for safety and
security. Ironically, they give up more safety and more security with every dollar they turn over to the bank. Additionally, depending on how your home is owned, when you die,
the equity in your home may even become subject to estate
tax. This is indeed a sobering thought.

The more money you put down, the more safety and security you create for the bank. Every dollar of principal that you
pay down gives the bank a slightly safer position with regard
to its real estate portfolio. The bank has a better chance of
getting its money out of a house with a lower mortgage than
a house with a larger mortgage. Think about it. If you have a
large equity position in your house, there is a greater likelihood that the bank will get its money if it has to foreclose
than if you had little to no equity in your house.

Any conceivable financial setback that might come your
way can be resolved more quickly if your home equity is separated from your property, rather than trapped in it. The
ideal solution is to be the owner of your own bank, borrow

---

1. "Compton Insurance Marketing", 2002.

from your bank, pay back your bank, save the interest and whenever possible, deduct the interest payments.

In a soft real estate market, home prices are based not on frenzied bidding wars, but simply on what people can really afford. As interest rates go up, home prices will likely come down. Wouldn't you rather have your equity separated from the value of your house? Or, would you rather give all of that money to the bank, so that it, and not you, can benefit from your hard-earned dollars?

For all of these reasons, a house fails the "good investment test." A house is not a *liquid* asset. A house can be very hard to sell, even in an overheated market. It is not a perfectly *safe* investment because the cost of housing can, and often does, go down, especially as interest rates go up. The equity you put into your house generates a rate of return of zero. I am not saying that you should not buy a home. Instead, you should not put more money into your house than you have to, and you should not pay off your mortgage any quicker than you are required to under the terms of the mortgage. Have the home, enjoy it and pay it off slowly. Put the money that you would have used to pay extra principal into a side fund. As will be discussed more in depth, a thirty-year mortgage is better than a fifteen-year mortgage, and an interest-only mortgage, where the interest rate is fixed for a specific period of time, is better than either of them.

Too Big To Fail

J. Paul Getty once said, "If you owe the bank one hundred dollars that's your problem. If you owe the bank one hundred million, that's the bank's problem." Sometimes the government will step in and save a business—an airline, an auto manufacturer, a bank—on the grounds that it is simply "too big to fail." In other words, if the business goes out of business, too many workers, families, investors, suppliers, customers or other individuals will be harmed. So, for the sake of society, it makes sense for the government to invest in keeping that business afloat.

The same principle applies to foreclosures in the world of home ownership. Let's say that Andrea and Bob live next door to each other in identical houses. Andrea owes $400,000 on her mortgage. Bob owes $100,000 on his because Bob has been regularly paying down his mortgage every month.

Now let's say that Andrea and Bob, for whatever reason, both fall three payments behind on their mortgage. Guess which mortgage the bank is going to foreclose on first?

Most people think the answer is Andrea's because when the bank forecloses, it will get $400,000.

That is not true. In a situation like this, the bank will foreclose on Bob's house first.

Why is that? Simply put, if the bank forecloses on Andrea's house and then sells it at auction or by some other means, there is no guarantee that the bank will get back all of its money. The real estate market might have gone soft or the house might have been over-mortgaged and there may be no way that a bank, or anyone else, could get $400,000 to satisfy the mortgage. The bank is very likely going to be more patient with Andrea, hoping that she finds a way to get back on her feet, so that she can continue her stream of mortgage payments on her over-valued or over-mortgaged house.

Now let's turn to Bob. Poor Bob. He did what his parents and his bank told him to do. He paid down his mortgage. Maybe he even took out a fifteen-year mortgage so that he could pay it off that much more quickly. Maybe he took advantage of that idea in the glossy bank brochure to make bi-monthly mortgage payments and thus owe less interest over the course of the loan. Or, maybe Bob took the advice that he heard on some financial talk show and made one additional mortgage payment every year, bringing his mortgage and interest payments down even faster.

Alas, all of Bob's conscientiousness is for naught. The bank does not care about your past. The bank only wants to know what you have done for it lately. If what you have done for it is missed three straight mortgage payments and if your house is worth well in excess of the remaining balance on the mortgage, you can count on the fact that the bank will foreclose on your house. Why shouldn't it? It is a sure thing for the bank—it will get every penny of the $100,000 it is owed.

Sorry, Bob. Maybe Andrea has a guest room for you.

Prepayment

New clients often tell me that they want to pay off their home loans. My response is always the same—"that is fine, but tell me why. What is the impetus underlying your desire to own your house free and clear?" Chances are, people look to pay off their house quickly to achieve security, peace of mind or increased cash flow. For our parents' generation, one of the most important and satisfying adult rites of passage was the "burning of the mortgage." Maybe your parents actually had a party to celebrate the occasion. They actually put a match to the mortgage documents (a few pieces of paper instead of the hundreds of pages of today's mortgages), secure in the knowledge that they now owned their house free and clear.

The world has changed. It is no longer in your best interest to own your house free and clear, no matter what your parents might have told you. The reality is, you do not achieve more safety and security when you pay off your home faster than required by the terms of your mortgage.

You know who really wants you to pay off your mortgage more quickly? Your bank!

If you have a thirty-year mortgage and you pay off your mortgage more quickly than you have to, you are essentially giving the bank money to which it really is not entitled, and you are giving it that money thirty years too early.

For example, when you buy a house for $1,000,000, and you put down twenty percent, you are essentially giving the bank an interest-free $200,000 loan. Your money is working hard for the bank. It puts the bank in a safer position. The bank is getting a return on your money while you get nothing. Every time you pay down your mortgage with greater than required payments, the bank receives the benefit of your money. The bank certainly does not reward you with interest. If the situation were reversed however—if the bank gave *you* some money (i.e. a mortgage or any other loan)—the bank would demand interest from you.

A fifteen-year mortgage carries a lower interest rate than a thirty-year mortgage. That is because the bank benefits by getting the money back sooner so it can loan out that money again. The bank gives you a slight break on the interest rate in order to encourage you to help it, the bank, avoid lost opportunity costs and increase it's chance to loan money out at higher interest rates in the future.

The most costly way to buy a home is to pay for it with cash and have no mortgage at all. The second most costly way is to have a shorter-term loan than a thirty-year mortgage. Having a mortgage with the longest possible term is the least expensive way to purchase a home. You must always consider what your money could be doing in other places within your personal economy. There are three important reasons why you need to make this consideration:

1. Your money will be available for other opportunities. If you tie up all of your cash in your home, you will invari-

ably miss out on great investment opportunities down the road. Why be house-poor when you can be cash-rich?

2. **You ultimately pay less tax.** Subject to government rules, you get to deduct the mortgage interest from your taxes.

3. **You pay less in inflation-adjusted dollars.** Do you have a fixed-rate mortgage? Inflation means that the dollar that goes to your mortgage ten or twenty years from now is worth only a fraction of the value of the dollar that you are paying today. Because of inflation, one dollar will be worth less in the future than it is today. So if you can postpone paying those dollars, even though it is still one dollar, it is a less expensive dollar in relative terms.

I am against prepaying mortgage loans. There is nothing to be gained by paying a mortgage down more quickly.

Every time you spend an extra one hundred dollars on your mortgage, you are in effect saying, "Mr. Banker, here is an extra one hundred dollars for you. Do not pay me any interest on this money. If I ever need it back, I will borrow it on your terms and at your interest rate and do not worry, I will prove to your team of investigators that there is a reason I should have it."

Prepaying your mortgage has major disadvantages:

• Your home costs more—you are paying more income taxes because you lose the interest deduction.

- Lost opportunity cost—you eliminate your return on potential investment dollars and lose to inflation.

- The bank, not you, gets control of your home equity.

- If you have to borrow against your home down the road, you will pay more in fees.

- Your foreclosure risk increases if you have to miss a few mortgage payments and you may be in danger of losing your equity altogether.

- You will probably get less money for your house if you have to sell it quickly because you will not have that "side fund" or cushion to tide you over through a financial crisis, and buyers smell desperation.

Some people say, "If I get a fifteen-year mortgage, I can pay the loan off that much more quickly."

Obviously, if you get a fifteen-year mortgage, it does get paid off more quickly. But let's consider the issue of safety for a moment. Let's say something bad happens to you or to the primary breadwinner in your family. Let's say that person becomes sick, injured, unemployed or the victim of a softening market. In that case, you are much better off having the equity of your house in a separate investment. That side fund you create will carry you through tough times. For most Americans, their house is their biggest investment. This means that most Americans are one car accident, work accident or job loss away from losing their homes.

Some people say that they want to get a fifteen-year mortgage because they can save one-half of one percent on the interest rate. But there are more tax deductions in the first fifteen years of a thirty-year mortgage than there are in an entire fifteen-year mortgage. By taking maximum advantage of the tax benefits you get in a thirty-year loan and investing in a side fund, you can pay off that thirty-year loan in less than fifteen years if at some point you make the emotional decision to do so!

Many people strive to have their house paid off by the time they retire. It is an admirable goal, but it is not really a sound financial goal. When you start taking money out of your qualified plan after you retire, that money is taxed as ordinary income. Even in retirement, you will want the tax deduction that comes from having a home mortgage. Otherwise, you will have been saving all that money in your qualified plan for all those years, just to give it to Uncle Sam.

To sum up, do not prepay your mortgage. If you do, you lose control of your money, you increase the cost of ownership of your home and you lower the return on your money. When you have a side fund—the money that you would have put into principal payments for your mortgage—you create more investment options for yourself and keep the valuable tax deductions you receive. You will also be safer and more liquid in the event of an emergency. The only entity that benefits from you paying off your loan more quickly is the bank. Do you want to be in the business of working long hours to enrich a bank?

The Bank's Best Interest

Let's take a look at the way banks work. Banks have a really sweet deal. They borrow money from you—the money you put into your checking, savings and money market accounts. Banks pay you anywhere between zero and five percent on the money they borrow from you, and charge you fees on everything from ATM use, to seeing a teller, to bouncing a check. What does the bank do with all the money that it has borrowed from you and people like you? Banks loan it out. They loan it out in the form of home loans at six and one-half percent per year, car loans at nine percent per year and credit card finance charges at twenty-one percent per year.

It gets even better for the bank. For every dollar in deposits that a bank takes in, the bank is allowed to loan out ten dollars. It is great to be a bank—banks borrow money for almost nothing and loan it out at high rates of interest several times over. This is the definition of a sweet deal indeed.

Banks have another great advantage; they get to "play the float." The float is the period of time between when the bank gets your money and when the bank has to give it back to you. Did you ever wonder why your bank makes you wait ten business days for an out-of-state check to clear, when they received the money electronically the day of your deposit?

The bank gets to make money on your money before they give it to you. When you deposit a check into a bank account, the bank has a policy on how many business days it takes for that check to clear. That policy has nothing to do with the amount of time it actually takes for the bank to receive the funds. The bank receives your money long before it makes it available to you in your account. This means that the bank gets to use your money for several days—for free—while you wait for your cash. It hardly seems fair, but it is the banks' game and the government makes the rules favoring the banks. Inevitably, you have to play by the rules that are slanted against you.

Wouldn't it be nice for you to be the bank for a change? Wouldn't it be nice to have the legal right to borrow large amounts of money at low interest rates and then turn around and loan out that money at significantly higher rates?

You can do it. You can be the bank. And all you need is a home mortgage.

Let's say that you have a mortgage on your home for $500,000. The natural inclination, fed by both what your parents told you and by what the banks are telling you, is to repay that money as fast as you possibly can. That way you will get to own your home outright.

Yet when you think about it, wouldn't it be better never to pay off that mortgage? After all, the bank is giving you $500,000 of that most coveted commodity, OPM (other people's money), and they are letting you have that money at the bargain basement price of somewhere around six and one-half percent per year. Uncle Sam, who has a vested interest in making sure that people own their own homes and pay property taxes, helps out by allowing you to deduct the interest on that loan from your gross income for income tax purposes. So that $500,000, at six and one-half percent interest, is actually only costing you about four percent per year.

What can you do with that money? Plenty. You may be able to invest in tax-free municipal bonds at four and one-half or five percent interest. You can find other real estate deals and make even more money. You can even invest in a business or purchase securities. There is absolutely no limit to the ways you can make money on the $500,000 that the bank was kind enough to loan you.

So the next time you hear anyone quoting William Shakespeare to the effect that we should neither be lenders nor borrowers, ask that person how Shakespeare would have felt about borrowing money for a home on Stratford-upon-Avon at an effective rate of four percent and making a six or seven percent return on that money. Even Shakespeare would have been impressed.

You should note, however, that banks lend out money not based on the underlying collateral—the house, the car or the boat—but based on your ability to repay the loan. Ironically, you have to prove to the bank that you do not really need the money before they are willing to give it to you!

Do you know the saying "What have you done for me lately?" No matter how much money you have paid a bank in the past, all the bank cares about is the next payment. If you are employed and in good health, the bank is happy to have you for a customer. What if something happens to you, to your job, to your health or to your ability to earn money? The bank is not interested in the fact that you have made nine years of payments without missing a beat. The bank's bottom line is whether or not you can make the next payment. And if you can't and are thinking of asking the bank for help, you are asking for help in the wrong place.

Lost Opportunity Cost

The amount of your mortgage payments dedicated to principal is treated the same way as your down payment—it is money that you do not ever get to see, touch, spend or draw interest on. It is simply an interest free loan to the bank. Your money is just gone—until you sell your house.

When talking about investments, you always want to consider opportunity costs. Your house, as an investment, is no different. Even the taxes you pay have lost opportunity costs. Every tax dollar from your pocket is a dollar that you cannot invest in something else that will benefit you. When you have the opportunity to make money on your money, you do not want to surrender that opportunity. When you pay off a home loan, you lose the opportunity to benefit from the leverage you gained when you borrowed that money, and you lose the tax benefit that came from having a mortgage.

Do I Hate Real Estate Or What?

The answer is NO! I do have very strong opinions on the issue of prepaying your mortgage, and I do believe that your home is a liability and not an asset until the day you sell it. But please do not misunderstand—real estate is an excellent investment. I heartily recommend buying investment properties. Real estate has tremendous tax advantages. For example, mortgage interest may be deductible; you may be able to deduct insurance and maintenance costs and depreciate the property. In addition, according to current law, real estate can pass income and capital gains tax efficiently because it provides a step-up in basis at death. If you own real estate, the key is to pay for it correctly.

Zero Percent Car Loans—Too Good To Be True

Things that seem too good to be true usually are. Take the so-called zero percent interest car loans. There is actually no such thing.

Here is how it works. You go to your friendly car dealer and ask how much a particular car costs. Instead of responding with a figure, the dealer asks, "How will you be paying for it? Cash or credit?"

You say, "I want to take advantage of that zero percent interest offer."

The dealer is delighted. "That is fantastic," he will say. "The price is $70,000. Do you want a forty-eight month loan, a sixty month loan, or a seventy-two month loan?"

Now let's say that you tell the dealer that you are going to pay cash for that same car. You will be quoted a very different price. "The cash price for the car is $66,000," the dealer will tell you. "It is actually $70,000, but we have a $4,000 cash-back bonus award."

In other words, the cost of the car is $66,000 to *everyone*, but there is a $4,000 penalty fee in case you want a so-called "zero percent interest car loan." The $4,000 is really a pre-payment of the interest.

Why do the automakers keep offering "zero percent interest" deals?

Because just about everybody falls for it.

Your Credit Card Company is Not Your Friend

I suspect that in a few years, credit card companies will completely halt the "float" that they currently provide their customers and start charging interest from the moment you make a purchase. But until that happens, they are finding more and more ways to squeeze money from their customers.

Say you buy a widescreen TV on January 1. Your credit card reporting period does not end until the twenty-fifth of the month, so essentially, you have a free loan from the credit card company for twenty-four days in the amount of the cost of the wide screen television. That is, unless you already have a balance on your card. If you have a preexisting balance, then you will pay interest at whatever rate the card charges you from the day you make your TV purchase (January 1).

Did you ever wonder why credit card companies are so anxious to make those zero percent loans? The answer is simple: so many credit card users will not be repaying their entire balance when it comes due, thus triggering interest rates that range from eighteen to twenty-one percent. In some states, interest rates are even higher.

At some point, credit card companies will decide that it is simply not worth making those free loans and will start charging you interest from the day you make your purchase. As a consequence, we may all be switching over to debit cards one hundred percent of the time. In any event, right now, if you leave an outstanding balance of even one dollar on your credit card, every purchase you make—until you pay off your balance in full—is subject to those eighteen to twenty-one percent (or higher) interest rates from the first day that you make the purchase.

Is that fair? No. Is that how they operate? You better believe it. The credit card companies are not your friends. They are in business to make money.

Part 8:
Spending

Sweet Dreams

Here is a question I always ask my clients:

"How much money do you need to have in a completely liquid environment so that you can sleep well at night, without worrying that a big bill could come in and bankrupt you?"

There is no one right answer to this question. Everybody has a different idea of how much money they want to keep liquid—and when I say liquid, I mean a money market account, a savings account or some other vehicle that would allow them to have all that cash in an instant if necessary. Below are some guidelines I offer my clients that can help you decide how much liquidity is "good liquidity" for you.

1. How much does it cost for you to live each month?

It is easy to figure out this information if you have Quicken, QuickBooks, Microsoft Money, the Living Balance Sheet or some other accounting software. After a few mouse clicks, you have your answer. Alternatively, you can simply look at your bank statement and get the information. The simple fact is that not everybody *wants to know* how much money they spend! Many people want to remain vague about exactly how much they have, how much they earn, how much they need, how much they spend and so on. For those people, a few simple mouse clicks can be tougher than climbing Mt. Everest. But you do need to know how much money you spend—you do have to face that fact. It is just as easy to overspend your income and assets whether you are making $50,000 a year or $1,000,000 a year. The starting point is knowing how much it costs you to live each month.

2. How secure is your job?

If you hold a public sector or government position like a schoolteacher or police officer, you have two things going for you—you have a regular salary and you have a great deal of job security. But most people who come to see me have jobs that do not always pay a specific salary. They may be entrepreneurs, business owners, realtors, stockbrokers or other individuals whose income is not always steady. People in this position need more liquid assets than those who know exactly how much money they can count on in any given month.

3. How many months worth of living expenses do you like to have in the bank?

This is the emotional piece, and it is different for everyone. The number of months worth of living expenses each person wants to have in the bank really comes down to the level of risk tolerance that different individuals possess. I usually advise my clients to keep at least three months worth of living expenses in a liquid environment—a savings account, a money market account or some other vehicle where access is easy and does not require the selling of an asset like a stock, a bond or a home.

Remember, money in the bank creates a lost opportunity cost for you because of taxes on its growth and the relatively low rate of return, so choose carefully. The trick here is the balancing act between the emotional need to have the money set aside and the knowledge that putting the money in a liquid environment means losing the opportunity to get a better after-tax rate of return on that money.

Where Did The Money Go?

Think back to college. It is Friday night, and you are lucky enough to have a twenty dollar bill in your pocket. You go out and you have a great time. On Saturday morning, as you are trying to reconstruct exactly where you were Friday night and what happened, you reach into the pocket of your jeans to see how much money you have left.

Two bucks—two crumpled up one dollar bills.

Where exactly did the money go and did I have a good time spending it?

Now fast forward to today. You are a successful individual, you and your spouse are making a lot of money, and it is Saturday morning. You look in your wallet or purse, and you wonder the same thing. I had a couple hundred in there on Monday; what did I spend it on this week?

We are a little older now and theoretically, we are a little wiser. But when it comes to spending, for most of us, not much has really changed. Instead of going down to the bar or club nearest the campus, we head out to the mall or the golf shop. And as the expression goes, "We spend money as if we had it."

Today we have the money to indulge in the sorts of high-level pleasures that were far beyond our means—or expectations—back when we were in college. What has happened for most of us is that our spending rose to the level of our income and often far beyond. Remember when your parents used to say, "Money burns a hole in your pocket!" It is sad but true—we let the amount of money in our wallet or purse dictate our spending level. In other words, the money we have drives our spending decisions. We need to be in control. So the question arises: How do you take control of your money?

I suggest an approach that makes investing automatic, protects your liquidity needs and acts as a brake on unconscious spending.

I call it the "Smart Account." A Smart Account is a completely liquid investment vehicle—a savings account or a money market account.

Here is how a Smart Account works. Every dollar you make goes directly into your Smart Account. Whether it is commission form a real estate sale or your salary or draw from your law firm or medical practice—however you make your money—it all goes straight into the Smart Account—every single dollar.

The minimum amount of money that you keep in your Smart Account is the amount that corresponds to your idea of good liquidity. Let's use the Jones family as an example. They have three young children in school, a home to maintain and the usual financial responsibilities that a married couple faces. Their monthly spending works out to about $15,000. They also save $5,000 per month. They would like to have three months of expenses in savings. Therefore, $45,000 is the minimum amount of money that the Joneses should keep in their Smart Account. Once a month, the Joneses write two checks from their Smart Account. The first check for $5,000 goes directly into a brokerage account. The second check for $15,000 covers family expenses for the upcoming month. The second check gets deposited into their home checking account and represents their monthly budget. Mrs. Jones, who does the shopping and bill paying, does so from their home checking account.

The Joneses understand that there are three months of the year during which they are likely to exceed their monthly budget. In September, there are new school expenses and activities to pay for. In January, there are holiday credit card bills to pay off and more extra curricular activities. In June, there will be expenses for the summer such as camp, summer activities and vacations. The Joneses do not meticulously maintain a ceiling of $15,000 on their spending every month. Some months will be a little higher, and some months will be a little lower. But with the Smart Account, they have what they need.

The Joneses have accomplished many of their security goals with their Smart Account. First, they have a consistent place to put their income, which will also make tax-time a lot easier. Second, they have an account in which they maintain appropriate liquidity for their family—three times their monthly expenses or $45,000. But it gets better.

Whenever the Joneses' Smart Account reaches $50,000, which is $5,000 *above* the amount of liquidity that they want to keep, the excess spills over and becomes invested automatically in a brokerage account. They have instructed the bank that whenever their account reaches $50,000, $5,000 is to be sent directly to their brokerage account. That brokerage account has a standing order to allocate any money that comes in from this account toward assets that they have pre-chosen—small cap versus large cap, individual stocks versus bonds and so on.

All of this happens automatically. The Joneses do not have to lift a finger to make these investments—it is all pre-arranged.

Why is this a great idea? As I mention elsewhere in this book, I often meet clients who have hundreds of thousands of dollars in money market accounts simply because they do not know where to put the money, and they are afraid that they are going to make a wrong investment choice. When you keep too much money in a money market account earning four percent, you are actually losing money. Remember, inflation is three percent per year, and after taxes the four percent the bank pays you works out to roughly two percent. Leaving too much money in a money market means that you are losing one percent per year on your money.

It is actually worse because not only do you lose the one percent to inflation, you also lose the lifetime value of what that money would have become had you taken it and invested it intelligently. The spillover order that the Joneses have with their bank, taking $5,000 out of that account every time the account reaches $50,000, ensures that they are not keeping too much money in an environment that is losing money after taxes and inflation.

How hard is it to create a "Smart Account" for yourself? It is incredibly easy. Open up a savings account at your bank and tell the bank exactly what number the account has to reach before the bank is instructed to spill over that extra money into a brokerage account or asset management account, either at the bank or with some other financial entity. Explain to your broker that money from your bank will be coming in periodically. Work with your broker to decide the best investments for your money.

Many of us are familiar with the adage, "pay yourself first." The wisest thing to do with income is to take a portion of it for savings and investment right off the top—before you pay any other bills. Unfortunately, most of us are not in the habit of maintaining that kind of discipline. It is much easier to set it up to happen automatically. In sum, there are six benefits of a Smart Account:

1. Easy tax record-keeping—all of your income goes into the same account.

2. Liquidity—you have all the money you need when you need it.

3. A simple and easy family budget—you do not have to monitor your spouse's spending, nor does your spouse have to monitor yours. As long as things stay within the monthly budget, a smart account will lead to conversations, not arguments, about where the money is going.

4. Automatic investment—you invest in the ways you have already thought through with your broker or investment advisor.

5. Protection—you are protected against the low rate of return of a bank account, losing money after taxes and inflation.

6. Curb on spending—you have an automatic check on spending during those excursions to the mall or the golf shop.

I think you can see why I call this account a "Smart Account"! I hope you will set up this type of account for yourself. It really works.

Liquidity—The Graduate Level Course

It is certainly a good idea to have liquid assets in case you have a sudden expense. But when you think about it, tying up $45,000—three times the monthly Jones family expenses—is not a great investment. Remember, after taxes the Jonses are only getting two percent on that money, so they are losing one percent after we consider inflation. As such, I would like to share with you a "graduate level" strategy for maintaining a reserve in case of a "rainy day."

Obtain a home equity line of credit in the amount of the liquid assets that you would normally want to keep—in the Jones' case, $45,000. Then, reduce the ceiling in your Smart Account to say, $20,000 instead of $45,000. Instruct your bank to start transferring money at a lower level. By doing this, you end up keeping a much smaller amount of money in your liquid account and directing more money into your investment portfolio where it can do much more for you.

If you use this strategy and you have an extraordinary expense, you can draw on your home equity line of credit to pay off the expense. The transfer made by your bank, once your Smart Account has exceeded $20,000, should then be redirected to the home equity line of credit until it is completely paid off. You can then resume investing the money. In other words, you are using other people's money to maintain your liquidity safety net. And best of all, it costs you nothing.

Couples And Money

When couples come to see me for the first time, there are a number of basic issues that predominate. A common issue is one spouse's concern over the other spouse's spending patterns. Often one spouse is looking for me to try to get the other spouse to spend less money.

I am not good at being "the heavy." Instead, I say to both spouses, "Let me show you a better way to keep track of your spending. Agree on a monthly budget and stick to it."

Nobody likes to have his or her spending patterns micromanaged. It does not feel good when a spouse says, "Are you going out for lunch with your friends *again?*" What I found in my own marriage, and in the experience of my clients, is that when one spouse writes a check for the monthly budget and the other spouse is responsible for paying the bills, the process removes a lot of the arguments about spending. If a couple goes over the budget, it normally leads to a conversation, not a fight, about the extraordinary expenses that month.

Another major concern that couples often have is that there are big bills and expenses coming due in the near future—college tuition for their children or retirement—and they are afraid that they will not have enough money. In those situations, the issue becomes finding innovative ways to save and invest so that those future expenses can in fact be met.

Sometimes spouses have different risk tolerances with regard to investment strategies. If we are talking about a brokerage account that both spouses own, our goal is to find a way to make them both happy and find a mutually acceptable risk level. Generally, the need is to satisfy the risk tolerance of the account holder, and if there are two holders, then both must be satisfied. If an account is in just one name, such as a 401(k) plan or an IRA, that problem usually does not exist.

Couples will often say, "We make a lot of money, but we do not save anything!" Those couples are the ones who most need to agree on a monthly budget and commit to sticking to it using the concept of the Smart Account. I suggest that people save at least fifteen to twenty percent of their income. Sometimes we have to start smaller. But once you get in the savings habit and you start to see the numbers increase in your investment vehicles, it really can be fun.

You Cannot Earn Your Way Out Of The Problem Of Overspending

Many people think, "If I just make X amount of dollars, I will have all I need!" The problem is that once we make X amount of dollars, we suddenly find ourselves in the social environment of people who make Y amount of dollars, or even Z amount of dollars. In other words, as our income goes up, so does our thirst for more and better things and hence, more spending. We want to drive a nicer car, belong to a club or a nicer club, take better trips and so on. When we do that, we brush up against people who make—and have—even more money.

Keeping up with the Joneses is a very expensive pastime. Even if our social circle does not change, our aspirations rise in excess of the rise in our income. When we make more money, we subconsciously tell ourselves that it is okay to spend more—sometimes to spend much more. This is how it happens that people can be earning a lot of money and yet have very little to show for it, except possibly some photographs of truly extraordinary vacations, wide-screen TVs or other accoutrements of affluent living.

Your Smart Account can help you keep your lifestyle from running away with your hard-earned dollars. Let's say that you have a better year this year than last year, and you make an additional $50,000 after taxes. You have a couple of options. The first option is that since you have an additional

$50,000, you go out and spend $60,000 or $80,000. Fortunately, there are some healthier alternatives.

Instead of simply spending to the wall or beyond, I recommend that you make a conscious decision to increase your monthly budget and live within those new means. For example, let's say your monthly budget was $15,000. On the fifteenth of every month, you have been writing a check for $15,000 from your Smart Account to your family checking account. Now you have $50,000 more in your account. You may consider increasing your monthly spending by $2,000. This means that on the fifteenth of the month, you will be writing a check for $17,000, and you can do a few extra, fun things with that additional $2,000. This accounts for $24,000, or slightly less than half of the $50,000 more you made this year. That leaves $26,000 flowing directly from your Smart Account to your brokerage account without any action or thought required on your part.

Yes, you can spend a little bit more, yet you are still saving more than half of the income boost.

Perhaps you want to spend all of the additional money. In that case, increase your monthly budget check to $19,000. This will eat up $4,000 a month or $48,000 of that additional $50,000 in income. When put in those terms, I think you will say to yourself, "Do I really want to do that? Do I really want to squander away my entire increase?"

There was an ad on TV a few years ago for an insurance company that showed the actual cost of a luxury item by comparing the cost of that luxury item, in this case a $6,000 watch, to the amount of money that could have been made over the next thirty years had that same $6,000 been invested "wisely" at six percent. The actual cost of that $6,000 watch was something more like $34,000 dollars. That is a whole lot more money than anyone thought they were spending on that watch.

If you say, "I had a great year, I am going to buy myself a $6,000 watch," the desire for spending is the only thing that is making your investment decision. If, on the other hand, you say, "I made an extra $50,000 this year; I am going to increase my monthly spending by X and save the rest," you are thinking in a much more balanced, sensible fashion. If you dedicated the first 3 months of your extra $2,000 a month to a kitty for that $6,000 watch, then you would be acting in an eminently more sensible fashion! The only problem is that your spouse may also have a good idea of what to do with that $6,000. So the race is on.

Crankshaft Envy

Let's talk about cars for a minute. Cars are the ultimate symbol of conspicuous consumption in our society. A comedian once said, "In Los Angeles, if four cars pull up to an intersection at the same time, the nicest car is allowed to go first. If all four people are driving the same car, the driver with the best hair gets to go first."

Even if you do not live in as car-conscious a place as Los Angeles, what you drive certainly reflects the image that you want to show the world. After all, if image were not a concern, we would all be driving Kias. Would you trust an investment advisor who drove a Kia?

I learned about this phenomenon first-hand. When I started in the business I used to drive a real piece of junk, an old Dodge Stratus. No one ever confused my Stratus with status! I was just never a car guy. I viewed a car simply as a means of transportation and not as a symbol of affluence. However, that was soon to change.

I remember one day when I went to visit a client and I parked my piece of junk in his driveway. He walked me out to my car at the end of our conversation, took a look at what was parked in his driveway and asked me a question. "Are you successful?"

"I am," I replied. And he asked me, "How do you define success?" I explained, "I make a very good living. I never miss any of my children's school events unless I want to, and I never work with anyone I do not want to work with. That is what success is for me."

"You don't look very successful in that car," my client said.

I did not think too much of that conversation until variations of it were repeated with other clients over the next few months. I realized that my clients wanted me to have a successful appearance—they wanted me to "dress the part," and that included the kind of car I drove. So I went out and I bought myself a nicer car—a Mercedes. I liked that car a lot and no one ever asked me about my definition of success after seeing my car.

As we make more money, we want nicer things. There is nothing wrong with that. I understand the way my clients feel as their net worths increase—I am right there with them. There will always be some new toy or trinket that suddenly becomes a possibility for you. When we buy a new home in a nicer neighborhood, our wants and desires increase because we see the cars and playthings of the people around us. When we go on vacations at nice places or join nice clubs, the same thing happens.

Author and social commentator Quentin Crisp once wryly observed, "Don't bother trying to keep up with the Joneses. Try to drag them down to your level." I certainly do not advocate that. What I am suggesting is that we live in a highly materialistic society, and the more we have, the more we want. The smartest thing we can do is to guard ourselves against the tendency to let our spending increase at the same rate as our income—or, as is so often the case, faster.

Part 9:
Strategies

No Bad Financial Products

There was a canine trainer who became famous for her expression, "There are no bad dogs." In other words, she was of the belief that any dog could be trained, as long as one took the proper approach.

Similarly, I like to say that there are no bad financial products out there. There are only bad strategies. It bears repeating: the overall goal of financial planning should be to live on more money now and pass on more money down the road. In order to achieve that goal, you need to have the right products working for you in the right ways. You need a great strategy to achieve financial balance. Diversification of assets takes into account the fact that all assets possess good and bad qualities. The proper strategy will allow you to leverage the good in any asset and eliminate, to the extent possible, the bad. This is true whether we are talking about mortgages, qualified retirement plans, real estate, stock market investments or even cash on hand. To accomplish financial balance, you should have a number of different pools of money, just as any great team has players who fill specific roles based on their individual abilities. For instance, a basketball team could not win with five point guards, nor could a football team win with eleven quarterbacks. When you have diversified assets working together as a team, you have a much greater chance of achieving financial success.

Contrary to popular belief, whole life insurance, used properly and combined with other assets, can actually make your other assets perform better. So please keep an open mind when considering the strategies suggested below. In this next section of the book, I outline strategies that will maximize your chances of financial success.

How To Improve Your Qualified Plan

Part 4 of this book outlined some of the problems associated with qualified plans. In sum, if you do not have an exit strategy from your qualified plan, it can be a taxation nightmare. Since most people's biggest fear in retirement is running out of money, they will not touch the principal in their qualified plan. Instead, they will attempt to live off of the interest generated by the plan. For wealthy individuals, this will cause financial devastation to their qualified plan.

When wealthy people die with qualified plans in their estates, assuming their applicable exclusions (the amount of assets that they can protect from federal estate taxes) are taken up somewhere else in their estates, their families may only receive between fifteen and twenty percent of the plans' proceeds. The remainder of any particular plan will likely go to Uncle Sam because it is subject to both estate tax and income tax. Additionally, if you only live off of the interest from your qualified plan, you will live on less money than you would have had you spent down the asset and systematically depleted the asset over time.

If, on the other hand, you had whole life insurance in addition to the qualified plan, the whole life insurance would provide a guaranteed death benefit to replace the qualified plan at your death, a cash value that you can tap if you deplete your plan during your lifetime, and a dividend that can provide you with an income stream for the rest of your life. Your whole life insurance then acts as a "permission slip" to spend your other assets differently and more efficiently. Therefore, you can live on more money while you are alive and still pass on more money at death.

What's In A Name?

I wish I could have been there the day that the insurance industry gave "whole life insurance" its name. I would have said, "What are you people THINKING???"

This may be the most poorly understood term in the entire financial industry. People might understand it better if it were called something like "amazing life insurance" or "fantastic life insurance" or, more to the point, "perhaps the best single asset you can possibly acquire because it offers you so many different ways to increase your financial net worth." I guess that is a little too wordy, so they settled on "whole life insurance." The problem with the name "whole life insurance" is that it does not explain what the product does. In this section, I want to explain exactly what whole life insurance does, because this information is vital to your financial future.

People seem to think, and I imagine that they have been improperly taught, that the only reason to have life insurance is to provide a sum of money at the death of the insured. Moreover, they believe that the only purpose for this sum of money is to either pay estate taxes or provide money to heirs. Purchasing life insurance solely to insure against an *early* death incorrectly presupposes that there is an age at which life insurance is no longer needed or necessary. This view could not be more shortsighted. In fact, the following are among the benefits that whole life insurance provides:

- Financial security—There are guarantees built into whole life insurance that cannot be taken away by a shift in market conditions. For instance, whole life insurance offers a guaranteed rate of return that does not include risk. The insurance can also provide disability protection. Specifically, if your contract contains a "waiver of premium" and you become disabled, the insurance is self-completing. This means that the insurance company makes the premium payments for you.

- <u>A forced savings plan</u>—Whole life insurance forces the owner to put away money on a regular basis.

- <u>Liquidity</u>—Whole life insurance provides the owner with a personal "bank" that can be tapped into or borrowed against. This also provides liquidity without the lost opportunity cost of putting money into a savings account.

- <u>Protection against lawsuits</u>—A whole life insurance policy is liability-proof in most states; no court can take it to satisfy a judgment against you.

Additionally, people incorrectly believe that if you "have to" buy life insurance, term life insurance is the "cheapest" form of life insurance available. In reality, this is not true. Term insurance is ultimately the most expensive type of life insurance you can buy. **Keep in mind that more than ninety-eight percent of all term life insurance policies never pay a claim.**[1] Thus, when you look at the real cost of the term life insurance, you must add to it the lost opportunity cost of making premium payments rather than investing that same money somewhere else. In the next few sections you will see how this works.

---

1. Penn State University, "1993 Study on the Fate of Term Insurance Policy."

The Easiest Way To Understand Whole Life Insurance

Let's say you are driving yourself to the airport to go on a one-week trip. You have a choice of two parking lots. The first parking lot charges $20. When you get back from your trip and you pick up your car, you must pay the parking lot attendant $140 to leave the parking lot with your car. The lot keeps the money, and you get your car back.

The second lot charges $100 a day—five times as much as the first lot. When you drop off your car you give the attendant $700. With this lot, however, when you get back, not only do you get your car, but you also get your $700 back, plus interest on your money.

Which lot would you pick?

Whole life insurance works like the second parking lot. You are not simply buying insurance. Instead, you have a product that pays you back, and when used correctly, can multitask, thereby making your other products work more efficiently.

Whole Life, Take A Bow

When you consider all of the guarantees and benefits that whole life insurance offers, it is hard not to be impressed. Here are just some of the highlights:

- A guaranteed death benefit and the piece of mind that comes along with it;

- A guaranteed premium—the insurance company cannot raise the premium for the life of the policy;

- A guaranteed cash value;

- A guaranteed minimum rate of return, which eliminates the risk that the cash value or death benefit will go down;

- Elimination of the lost opportunity cost associated with term life insurance;

- A guarantee that once a dividend is declared, it cannot be taken away;

- A permission slip (created by the guaranteed death benefit, cash value and declared dividends) to spend down other less efficient assets;

- An improvement in the way other assets in your economic system perform. This means that whole life insurance has a return external to that achieved by the life insurance itself;

- Cash value that grows in a tax-deferred manner and can be accessed non-taxably if done correctly;

- A policy that can keep pace with inflation if dividends are used to purchase paid-up additional insurance. This will increase both the cash value and the death benefit of the policy;

- A policy that is liquid and allows access to the cash value either by surrendering it or borrowing from it. Any declared dividend can also be used as an income stream to enhance your lifestyle. If you borrow from the policy, you are not required to pay back the loan. You can also use your cash value as collateral for a bank loan;

- A cash value which is exempt from creditors' claims—it is liability-proof in most state; and

- A policy that can also include a waiver of premium; this means that if the insured becomes sick or injured, the insurance company will pay the premium for them.

In light of all of these benefits, the inclusion of whole life insurance makes any financial plan work more efficiently. Moreover, you would be hard-pressed to make up for its absence with any other financial product or combination of products. In fact, the only drawback to whole life insurance is that it takes two to three years to build up steam. In most policies, the cash value does not begin to accrue appreciably until the policy has been in force for a couple of years. Thus, whole life insurance is neither a quick fix nor a short-term financial product.

Whole life insurance has many great attributes, such as a guaranteed rate of return on the cash value, a liquid side fund that you can borrow at a guaranteed fixed interest rate and a guaranteed death benefit that creates an estate for your heirs or a charity. However, one of the most important benefits whole life insurance gives you is economic certainty. The whole life insurance contract guarantees allow you to make economic decisions based on the most efficient use of your money rather than refraining from those decisions because you are scared that you will run out of money during your lifetime.

A Great Team Player And A Superstar

In sports, a superstar is an individual capable of helping his teammates reach even higher levels of greatness. Michael Jordan, Jason Kidd and Kobe Bryant all have this gift.

You can think of whole life insurance in that same category—it is an asset that makes all of your other assets perform better.

What makes whole life insurance such a superstar?

In some respects, it is better than municipal bonds because typically, the rate of return on cash value is higher than the return on municipal bonds over the long term. Additionally, whole life insurance provides a death benefit to boot. Moreover, if used properly, whole life insurance has similar income tax advantages to those of municipal bonds. Whole life insurance is better than corporate bonds because if done properly, the returns you make on whole life insurance do not generate taxes. Thus, whole life insurance can be used to satisfy the "fixed income" part of your portfolio. Also, the fact that whole life insurance is a "non-correlated" asset, i.e. it is not as reliant on the market as other fixed income investments, provides an added layer of diversification and safety. Finally, whole life insurance can be better than real estate because real estate is not liquid, and despite the go-go years of the early 2000s, the upward trends in real estate are simply not guaranteed.

For all these reasons, I firmly believe that whole life insurance is a true star performer. This does not mean, however, that you should not have those other assets. It just means that whole life insurance can help you achieve financial balance so that you can live on more money and pass more money on when you are gone.

So, how does whole life insurance—your financial superstar—make the rest of your assets perform better?

As I discussed earlier, if you have a qualified plan, from a tax perspective, it is better to spend it down in your lifetime than to pass it on to your heirs. Money invested in your qualified plan can be subject to severe income and estate taxes. When you have whole life insurance, you have a permission slip to spend down your qualified plan money in your lifetime because you still have the guaranteed cash value of your whole life policy, the dividends and the death benefit.

The same thing is true for your non-qualified investments—your stocks, bonds and mutual funds that are held outside of your qualified plan. It is more efficient to spend down these assets in retirement than it is to pass them through your estate where Uncle Sam is sure to gobble up a huge chunk. I cannot reiterate enough that whole life insurance is a permission slip to spend down those investments as well.

With a whole life insurance policy, you have the ability to obtain a reverse mortgage on your home. The mortgage can be paid off at death with the insurance proceeds if your heirs so desire.

Whole life insurance can even help with your disability protection. If you were out of work due to a major disability, no one would say, "Since you are such a great person, we are going to keep on paying all of your obligations." But when you have whole life insurance, there is the potential of obtaining a disability waiver of premium. If you purchase the waiver and you become disabled, the insurance company will make your payments for you. Not a bad deal.

Put it together—the high-performance aspects of whole life insurance combined with the fact that it makes the rest of your investments perform better—and you can see why I call whole life insurance a superstar.

Debunking Some Myths About Whole Life Insurance

Let's take a look at some of the biggest myths that have come to surround whole life insurance.

"How do I know it works?"

Whole life insurance has actually been around longer than term life insurance! Whole life insurance was originally introduced in the 1860's, while term insurance did not make its first appearance until the 1940's. For more than sixty years, big companies like General Electric have been using whole life insurance to keep their companies safe, while giving perks to their top executives.

Additionally, the United States General Accounting Office found in its 2004 study, that many of the largest banks in the United States count cash value life insurance as a "tier one" asset.[2] For banks, tier one capital is "a measure of the equity cushion that banks have available to absorb loss."[3] Moreover, the General Accounting Office found that of the banks that owned life insurance, the cash surrender value generally accounted for twenty-five percent of their tier one capital.[4] If whole life insurance is good for the top executives at GE and the country's largest banks, why wouldn't you consider it for yourself?

"Everybody says it is a rip-off."

Whenever "everybody" is saying the same thing, you can pretty much count on the fact that the herd mentality is in effect. When was the herd ever right about anything? After all, the herd went into oil and gas in the 1980s just before it tanked, bought Internet stocks before the NASDAQ burst, went deeply into WorldCom, Tyco, Global Crossing and

2. United States General Accounting Office, Report to Congressional Requesters, "Business-Owned Life Insurance—More Data Can Be Useful In Making Tax Policy Decisions," Released May 2004.
3. United States General Accounting Office, Report to Congressional Requesters, "Business-Owned Life Insurance—More Data Can Be Useful In Making Tax Policy Decisions," Released May 2004.
4. United States General Accounting Office, Report to Congressional Requesters, "Business-Owned Life Insurance—More Data Can Be Useful In Making Tax Policy Decisions," Released May 2004.

Enron before those companies all imploded and most recently bought a lot of real estate.

In short, anytime the herd is headed in one direction, you want to get out of their way before you get trampled! The herd also believes that it is best to pay off your house and give the bank tens or hundreds of thousands of dollars of your hard-earned money before the bank is entitled to that money. It bears repeating: the herd is not usually right. Don't follow the herd into the slaughterhouse!

Additionally, the media, who may have other reasons for steering people away from whole life insurance, guides the herd. For instance, if you purchase whole life insurance, you may have less money to allocate toward financial instruments like mutual funds. Thus, publications whose advertisers are mostly mutual fund companies would not support whole life insurance.

"Why buy something expensive when you can buy something more cheaply?"

The same people who espouse, "buy term and invest the difference" would laugh in your face if you told them to "buy a Kia instead of a BMW and invest the difference" or "live in the smallest, cheapest home you can find in the worst neighborhood in town and invest the difference." The simple fact is that we buy a lot of things that are high quality, even though less expensive alternatives exist. Quite frankly, we work hard so we can have those choices! What ever happened to, "You get what you pay for"? The reason we hate that expression is that it interferes with the basic human motivation called *greed,* which means we want something for nothing.

Why do you drive a nice car? Why do you live in a nice home? Wear nice clothes? Go to fine restaurants and stay at nice hotels? Play great golf courses? Drink the best Scotch?

In one word: value.

Value has its price.

Being The Donald

If you ever suspected that the way Donald Trump buys real estate is very different from the way most Americans buy real estate, you are absolutely correct. The average American who wants to purchase a house or a commercial building has to make a down payment which represents a percentage of the total purchase price. Real estate moguls like Trump, however, do not use their cash to provide a down payment. Instead, they leverage their other assets. They use equity from one building to buy another, and they use the cash flow from one building as a means of making mortgage payments on another building. This gives these moguls the ability to buy building after building without taking a dime out of their own pockets.

The good news is that if you have whole life insurance, you have the very same option. You can pledge the cash value of your policy to the bank to use as a down payment to buy a building.

Let's say you want to buy a building for $1,000,000. You could borrow the first twenty-five percent of the money from your whole life insurance policy and then obtain a mortgage for the remainder of the purchase price. If that building generates a $24,000 a year positive cash flow after paying all of the expenses related to the building, such as interest, taxes and maintenance, what is the effective rate of return on that investment? The answer is that the rate of return is infinite because you did not use any of your own money to make the purchase. You used the best type of money to implement the strategy—other people's money (remember OPM).

If you wanted to establish your own bank, it would take about three years, untold legal fees, tremendous paperwork and red tape just to get a charter from the government. With whole life insurance, by the time you have made three years' worth of premium payments, you will have a "bank" of money from which you can borrow without having to prove yourself worthy of the loan.

And it is a lot cheaper than hiring lawyers!

Free BMWs! Right This Way!

One of my associates wanted to drive a new BMW. He looked into the cost of leasing the car and when he saw that the payments were higher than he wanted to pay, he looked into the possibility of buying it. My friend, however, did not want to tie up the amount of cash necessary to buy the car outright, and he did not want to be responsible for lease payments (at the end of which he would have nothing to show for the money he had spent). Putting the car purchase on hold, he decided instead to buy a building. He took a loan from his whole life insurance, and he used that money as the down payment on a new building. He used the down payment plus a bank loan to buy the property. Now that building produces a positive income stream sufficient to buy or lease his subsequent new cars. By using his life insurance to purchase an investment property that produces an income stream, he can now lease or buy any car he wants.

It sure beats making car payments!

College Funding

As discussed earlier in this book, funding a college education with a 529 plan or a similar strategy is an inefficient approach. It is the essence of "save and spend"—we put a lot of money into a savings vehicle only to spend that money before it has a chance to really grow as an investment. In business this is typically referred to as a sinking fund. Whole life insurance is a great way to help with college funding. You can utilize whole life insurance to pay for college in a number of ways. First, you could borrow the money for college by obtaining a mortgage and then make the mortgage payments from the dividends from the life insurance. That way, you may be able to deduct some of the interest costs. Second, you can borrow from the life insurance to pay for college and keep your money growing on the exponential curve.

Using a whole life insurance strategy to help fund college may also avoid disqualifying your child from loans, grants and aid programs. If there is money in your child's name, or even in a 529 plan, your child may be barred from participating in assistance programs. In effect, this punishes you for your diligence.

Keep in mind that there is also a chance that your child may not go to college or that he or she may get a scholarship. In either event, there is a lost opportunity cost to the money you saved for college. Instead, with the whole life insurance funding method, you have options and options are powerful. Whole life insurance is also self-completing in that if you die or become disabled before you finish funding the education, the life insurance will complete the task.

Do Not Thank Me, Thank The Neighbors!

Wouldn't it be great to send your kids to school and have someone else pay for it? Wouldn't it be even better to then get a tax deduction for the tuition payments on top of it? The least efficient way to send your kids to school is the "save and spend" method that I discussed earlier. Keep in mind that with virtually every investment, the investment curve—the rate at which the investment increases in value—stays flat for a long time and then, through the magic of compounding of interest, gets steep. The problem with the "save and spend" approach is that you typically sell the investment before you get to the really steep part of the curve. You never want to jump off the curve with a successful investment because when you get back on the curve, you must wait through the flat years until the curve gets steep again.

Let me suggest a much better way to send your kids to college. Take out a home equity line of credit on your home to pay the tuition bills. This will give you a tax deduction for the interest that you are paying. It will also allow you to use other people's money to pay those tuition bills. You can then pay back that loan with inflated dollars so your actual out-of-pocket cost will be lower. The money that you borrowed can also be paid back either out of pocket or by using the dividends from your whole life insurance.

When your kids come to thank you for paying for their college tuition (hopefully not an unlikely event), you will be able to say, "Don't thank me! Thank this great country of ours!" After all, the fact that you are able to use other people's money to pay for your children's college tuition, together with the tax deductions that you get for paying the tuition bills, makes this strategy a truly beautiful one.

Part 10:
Estate Planning

Estate Planning ... The Basics

Most people create an estate plan to ensure that, upon their death, their assets are transferred according to their wishes as efficiently as practicable and with as little tax implications as possible. Thus, your estate plan should outline several key points. Your estate plan should:

- Enumerate what assets you have and where they are, so that your executor can collect them efficiently;

- Describe how your assets should be distributed. This means that the plan will make sure that the assets are distributed the way you want them to be distributed. You can dictate to whom the assets go, when the assets go and what has to be done in order for the assets to be transferred; and

- Seek to protect your assets from estate taxes, income taxes, costs and fees.

Like the inventory you should keep of the contents of your home (discussed in Part 6), you should also keep an inventory of your assets. This will make it easier for the person who is responsible for collecting your assets at death. Also, this will protect you if something unforeseen happens to you and you are unable to adequately administer your own affairs. There are several computerized tools on the market today that can help you with this task. You should look for a "data aggregation" tool that will periodically and automatically update your information. Your financial planner should be able to provide such a tool for you, and if he cannot, feel free to contact my team.

At death, all of the assets that are in your estate must pass through probate (under the jurisdiction of the local probate court), and probate costs must be paid. Conversely, assets that are not in your estate do not pass through probate.

One way to avoid probate is by utilizing trusts where appropriate. A trust is a legal entity created to hold assets and provide for the efficient distribution of those assets. There are many types of trusts including, but not limited to, life insurance trusts, living trusts, grantor trusts and special needs trusts. Trusts must be set up by legal professionals. If structured and used properly, trusts are an excellent way to control and pass assets.

Since the goal of estate planning is to pass your assets efficiently (i.e. quickly and with as little tax consequences as possible), how you own your assets is of paramount importance.

As discussed in Part 6 of this book, every person is entitled to an "applicable exclusion" which is the amount of assets that they are allowed to protect from federal estate taxes. Therefore, you should align your estate in such a way that you and your spouse have enough assets in your individual names to each take advantage of this exclusion.

As with your financial plan, your estate plan needs to be coordinated. There are many assets that your will does not control. These include, but are not limited to, your life insurance and your qualified plan. Both of these assets have beneficiary designations that operate outside of your will. For instance, if your will leaves all of your assets to your spouse and the beneficiary designation on your life insurance names your brother as the primary beneficiary, then your brother—not your spouse—would get the death benefit from your life insurance. This is of utmost importance when insurance proceeds or qualified plan assets are left directly to children. These children may no longer be minors, but nonetheless, you may not want them to inherit the money until a later age. Even if your will sets up a trust for your children, your life insurance may pass outside of your will and go to them directly if your beneficiary designations are not coordinated with your will.

It is important to create a great estate plan because you can save your family a tremendous amount of taxes, time and energy. In addition, creating an estate plan enables you to dictate under what conditions your assets transfer. I cannot stress enough the importance of having a plan that is reviewed regularly; only with proper planning and review can you create a plan that will endure changing laws and the test of time.

Family Limited Partnerships (FLP) and Limited Liability Companies (LLC)

There is an expression that says, "from pauper to wealth to pauper in three generations." That statement has never been more true. Generally, wealth that takes one or two generations to create, vanishes within a generation or two. This is not because the heirs are spendthrifts or lazy or demotivated by their wealth, but because the taxman takes it away.

I would like to share a very successful strategy for keeping money where it belongs—in the family.

Let's take the case of a couple that has extensive real estate holdings but no estate plan. This scenario happens all of the time. When a couple like this comes to me, I draw a circle on a piece of paper. In the middle of the circle I put the letter E, which stands for their estate. I then draw a line down the middle of the circle, bisect the E and color in half of the circle.

"The half of the circle that is in color," I explain, "goes to your heirs. The rest goes to Uncle Sam." I then ask my client, "How do you feel about that?" Without fail, their response includes varying displays of colorful language.

I then point out that estate taxes are due nine months after death. This means that their children will be forced to sell properties quickly in order to generate the money necessary to pay the estate tax. I ask them how they feel about *that*. Needless to say, they do not like that either.

Then I say, "Isn't that the kind of deal you just love as a buyer? The situation where the seller is absolutely forced to sell and you can swoop right in and buy for a rock-bottom price?" Finally, I get a smile. They love those deals!

"But the problem now," I point out, "is that your kids are the forced sellers. Is that what you want for them?"

Of course not.

One excellent solution to this dilemma is to create a Family Limited Partnership (FLP) or a Limited Liability Company (LLC). These are legal entities that exist outside of your estate and allow you to retain control over the assets within them. When a person with an FLP or LLC dies, if the FLP or LLC has been established properly, the assets in the FLP or LLC transfer to the next generation, or to whomever is "inheriting" those assets, in a much more tax efficient manner. No forced sales. Your holdings stay intact.

Real estate is not the only thing that can go into an FLP or an LLC. They can also hold life insurance, appreciated assets (like stocks) or just about any other asset. They are very flexible and effective tools. The reason more people do not use FLPs or LLCs is simply because they get overwhelmed by information. They are afraid to sit down and find out exactly how they work.

As I like to say, you can open your mind to new ideas now, or, you or your heirs can open your wallet to the IRS later. It just makes sense to know all of the options available to you instead of sticking your children with the unpleasant task of having to pick and choose which of your most treasured holdings they will sell quickly in order to satisfy the demands of estate tax.

One of the relatively few downsides to FLPs or LLCs is that the laws regulating them can change. But, as with anything regulated by the government, the laws can change. This issue, in and of itself, is not sufficient enough to disregard using these strategic tools. They do cost money to establish, but the amount of money that you can save—in the millions or tens of millions of dollars, depending on your estate, makes that investment in legal fees a very small one indeed. Equally important is to choose the right attorney. Make sure to choose an attorney who is well versed in the creation and maintenance of FLPs or LLCs.

These vehicles are simple from a conceptual point of view—it is a basket in which to place assets in order to keep them out of your estate but over which you can maintain control. From a legal point of view, however, they are rather complicated, so you want to make sure that your attorney really knows what he or she is doing. FLP's and LLC's are outstanding ways to preserve wealth; I urge you to look into them further if you want to keep your money where it truly belongs—with those you love.

Family limited partnerships and limited liability companies are just two of several advanced estate planning techniques that can drastically reduce estate taxes. There are many more. I encourage you to investigate them or work with someone who is well versed in this area. They are however, beyond the scope of this book. Feel free to contact me or my team if we can be of service in this area, even if it is just to point you in the right direction.

Part 11:
Conclusion

If Everybody Is Doing It, It Is Probably A Bad Idea

One of the themes that runs through the material I have shared with you is that if everyone you know is following a particular financial strategy, there are only two possibilities. One is that you surround yourself with individuals who are highly astute when it comes to their financial decisions, and you are justified in heeding their advice. The other, and more likely possibility, is that your friends are following the crowd, and when it comes to making financial decisions, the crowd is usually wrong.

Keep in mind that if the overwhelming majority of people are following any particular strategy, then somebody else is benefiting more than they are from their use of that strategy. That "somebody else" may be a mutual fund company, an insurance company, a brokerage house, Uncle Sam or some combination thereof. There is no "one size fits all" when it comes to investing. A strategy that might work wonderfully for an individual making $40,000 a year is probably a terrible strategy for you. Just because an idea is ubiquitous does not mean it is wise.

There is an expression on Wall Street—"bulls and bears make money and pigs get slaughtered." This means that individuals who put effort into their financial lives generally improve their situations, but those who are tempted by greed often meet a sad end. To this metaphor I would like to add one twist: sheep get shorn. In other words, investors who act like sheep and do what everybody else is doing just because they are doing it, tend to end up getting fleeced. I am not suggesting that the mutual fund industry is out to get you or that the insurance industry does not have your best interest at heart. As discussed earlier, there really are no bad financial products. It is just that there are bad strategies. Using a financial product that is incorrect for you or using a financial product the wrong way is going to have negative ramifications on your net worth.

Bottom line: if everyone you know is zigging, it is almost certainly time to zag.

Rules To Live By

I have two basic rules when it comes to guiding my clients, and your financial planner should live by them too:

Rule #1: You cannot employ a strategy that I show you unless you can explain it back to me.

Rule #2: I will not do something for you if you can do it more cost effectively elsewhere.

Let's take a closer look. Rule #1—you cannot do it with me if you cannot explain it back to me—boils down to "never invest in something you do not understand."

The last thing I want is for one of my clients to be at a cocktail party trying to explain their portfolio or a strategy to someone and not be able to explain their reasoning for why they got into, or out of, a particular investment. I do not want them saying, "I am not sure why, but Mitch said it was a good idea!"

Anything that they cannot explain back to me is probably too complicated for them. If it is too complicated an investment to explain, then they will not know the best ways to use it or when to properly exit the investment.

Rule #2—I will not do something for a client if they can do it less expensively elsewhere—boils down to my goal of getting my clients in the best financial position possible. A seventy-year-old man who had immigrated to the United States as a young man came to me. He had done everything the right way. He was frugal, used coupons, lived below his means—he did everything that the rest of us never manage to accomplish!

As a result, he had socked away an impressive $2,100,000 in his retirement plan. The government pension program in which it was invested offered a guaranteed eight and one-quarter percent on that money.

I asked him, "What can I help you with?"

"I want ten percent," he replied.

"Why," I asked amazed, "would you want to incur more risk to make an additional one and three-quarter per-cent—when you have already won the game?"

This guy had done the right things all of his life, and now he was willing to blow it all, just to make that additional one and three-quarter percent. I would not be a party to that. I told him that if he really wanted to make a riskier investment that had a slight possibility of a marginally higher payoff, he would have to do it with someone else.

Why would anybody want to get ten percent with tremen-dous risk when they could get eight and one-quarter percent with no risk?

The answer boils down to one simple word: greed. He was living the American Dream and now he was on the verge of succumbing to greed. This is the biggest threat the truly affluent face.

Sometime later, I checked in with him. I was pleased to see that he had taken my advice and had kept his money exactly where it was.

Talk about winning the game.

Further illustrating Rule #2, there are certain investments that do not require someone in my position to oversee. For example, take an individual who wishes to day-trade in the stock market. My securities license permits me to trade on my client's behalf, but it is much more cost-effective for my clients to do their own day trading without involving me. If I am not providing value or if it would cost more to do the same thing with me than without me, I advise my clients to do it without me. I believe that any self-respecting financial strategist should do the same.

Parting Words

I wrote this book to share my ideas with others. I truly love to see people succeed. I find that the ideas that I have shared with you in this book resonate most deeply with people who share a common set of characteristics:

- They are future thinking. They have the ability to envision a future that is bigger than their present (even though their present is pretty nice).

- They have integrity. They know when to push the envelope, but they would never go so far as to cheat or do anything illegal.

- They care about their family. They want to do the best that they can to provide for their future.

- They have a little bit of humility about their financial lives. They recognize that they are really good at what they do, but they also understand that they do not know everything about protecting and growing their wealth. They are smart and fully capable of making the right decisions once they are informed of their choices, but they realize that they may not know all of the choices currently available to them.

If these characteristics describe you, then I hope that this book becomes a starting point for you toward a more engaged conversation about good strategic financial planning. If winning the game of life at a very high level is important to you and if you find these ideas as exciting as I do, then you are truly on the path to living better and achieving your life goals.

Good luck!

978-0-595-49492-7
0-595-49492-7

Printed in the United States
203848BV00002B/130-1023/P